STUDIES IN SOUL TENDING

OR

PASTORAL WORK IN ITS RELATION TO THE
INDIVIDUAL

BY THE LATE
F. J. B. ALLNATT, D.D., D.C.L.

CANON OF THE CATHEDRAL OF THE HOLY TRINITY, QUEBEC
HARROLD PROFESSOR, AND DEAN OF THE FACULTY OF DIVINITY,
BISHOP'S UNIVERSITY, LENNOXVILLE, CANADA
AUTHOR OF "THE WITNESS OF ST. MATTHEW"

EDITED BY
G. ABBOTT-SMITH, D.D.

"Διὸ μελλήσω ἀεὶ ὑμᾶς ὑπομιμνήσκειν περὶ τούτων, καίπερ εἰδότας, καὶ
ἐστηριγμένους ἐν τῇ παρούσῃ ἀληθείᾳ"—2 ST. PET. i. 12.

LONDON
SOCIETY FOR PROMOTING
CHRISTIAN KNOWLEDGE
NEW YORK AND TORONTO: THE MACMILLAN CO.
1922

TO THE MEMORY OF

THE AUTHOR'S VALUED FRIEND

J. M. P.

FOREWORD

THE literature of Pastoral Theology has grown apace of late and, with the addition of some recent works, begins to approach a completeness of treatment which the growing sense of its importance more and more insistently calls for. There is still room, however, for special presentation of particular aspects and departments of the subject, such as the care of the individual soul, including that of the priest himself, with which it is the aim of this short treatise to deal.

On the subject-matter of these Studies, the author was peculiarly well fitted to speak from a long experience both as Parish Priest and Lecturer in Theology. In both of these relations, within the sphere of his influence, he occupied a position almost unique in Canadian Church life during the greater part of the last half-century.

In these pages the judicious reader will observe an independence of treatment which, if in part removed from some of the more prevalent currents of present-day thought and practice, reveals a rich spiritual experience, a profound knowledge of human nature, and a fine insight into " the deep things of God."

The editor's labours have been reduced to a minimum by the work already done on the manuscript by the Rev. R. J. Shires, B.D., sometime tutor at Bishop's College and a former pupil of Dr. Allnatt's. As a labour of love, Mr. Shires undertook to type the whole work, most of it at the author's dictation, and it is due to the painstaking care which he has given to its arrangement that the manuscript appears in a fairly complete form for publication. The fact that the work was unfinished accounts for the abruptness of its conclusion, and also for the form of some of the sentences which appear just as they were dictated, but which would doubtless have been somewhat recast by the author with his accustomed care and exactitude.

It had been Dr. Allnatt's intention to complete the work himself in the summer of 1920, but God willed otherwise, calling him to higher service, and it remained for other hands to give it some finishing touches and send it forth as a small memento of a singularly rich and fruitful life, and as a last message to those who knew and loved him as well as, it is hoped, to a wider circle, from a faithful priest and servant of the Lord, who herein "being dead, yet speaketh."

G. ABBOTT-SMITH.

MONTREAL,
    Easter, 1922.

PREFACE

THE suggestions which are embodied in the following pages are the outcome of many years of intimate association with divinity students and young clergymen during their period of preparation for the priesthood. The "Studies" are in great measure founded upon lectures delivered upon the subject of Pastoral Theology in some of its departments. Their publication in the present form is the result of kindly pressure on the part of valued friends, who were of the opinion that there was something about them which seemed to promise a possibility of their meeting certain needs incident to the earlier stages of the priestly life.

As their title implies, they make no claim to be regarded as a complete or connected system of direction on the subjects with which they deal ; nor do they profess to include the whole range of aspects under which any particular subject is capable of being regarded. They amount, in fact, to not much more than certain haphazard suggestions with reference to various features of clerical life and work which happen to have been brought to my attention as subjects of inquiry, or which have suggested themselves to me as seeming to call for special notice.

This explanation may account for what might otherwise appear to be inexplicable omissions, as well as for the comparatively slight treatment of subjects, of which a fuller consideration would perhaps be expected.

If some of the suggestions appear trite, my plea is to the effect that reasons for their introduction have been found in the fact that, in some form or other, they have been brought before my notice as calling for attention.

On the other hand, if some suggestions appear novel, and open to objection on that account—possibly also as intrinsically of a character at variance with current thought—I may in this case plead that my purpose is to offer suggestions with reference to provision for serious needs, or to promote important ends, which perhaps are not at present fully provided for. And while I am far from presuming to insist upon the superiority of my own proposals to those which might be made, I would, nevertheless, offer them for consideration with a view of inviting the suggestions of others which may possibly be better worth adoption.

The consideration of the Divine Immanence, or the Real Presence of God in the Person of the Logos, as manifested in the external world of nature—in relation to the place which this consideration should take as a factor in the formation of the devotional habit—is a subject which, I think, has hardly yet received the attention to which its importance would seem to entitle it, and which the advanced stage of thought which characterises the present day would appear to demand. I have, therefore, offered a few suggestions on this subject, and trust that they may not be regarded as out of place in this connection.

In all their incompleteness, and with all their defects, I commend these " Studies " to the members of the Divinity Classes, among which—albeit so imperfectly, yet taking it all in all, so happily—I have so long been privileged to labour.

F. J. B. A.

CONTENTS

PART I

THE PRIEST'S CARE FOR HIS OWN SOUL

PART II

THE PRIEST'S CARE OF THE SOULS UNDER HIS CHARGE

PART I

THE PRIEST'S CARE FOR HIS OWN SOUL

His nurture of it, to sustain its capacity for the nurture of others.

"Ταῦτα μελέτα, ἐν τούτοις ἴσθι,
ἵνα σοῦ ἡ προκοπὴ φανερὰ ᾖ πᾶσιν.
ἔπεχε σεαυτῷ, καὶ τῇ διδασκαλίᾳ.
ἐπίμενε αὐτοῖς
τοῦτο γὰρ ποιῶν καὶ σεαυτὸν σώσεις καὶ τοὺς ἀκούοντάς σου."

1 Tim. iv. 15 16.

STUDIES IN SOUL TENDING

INTRODUCTION

A TREATISE upon pastoral work can hardly enter upon its subject without a word by way of emphasising the warning so often repeated—and apparently so obvious as to seem almost superfluous—against the danger on the clergyman's part of undertaking to help others to do what he has not yet done for himself.

That a man who has never experienced the love of Christ (the first requisite), as his own possession, should take upon himself to do Christ's work, and be the means of instilling that love into the hearts of others, must unavoidably imply a life actuated by hypocrisy of the most serious kind. Unavoidably, because the very fact of his undertaking the charge of others in this respect is necessarily understood by them as implying the assurance that he is himself in the condition into which it is his avowed purpose to bring them. Were it otherwise they would simply scout the idea of his occupying the position which he has assumed.

It would be difficult to find a passage of Scripture expressive of such utter sadness—amounting almost to a wail of despair—as that in the Song of Songs : " They made me keeper of the vineyards ; but mine

3

own vineyard have I not kept."[1] It may be well, therefore, at the outset of our subject, to suggest a few thoughts with the view of aiding the young clergyman in his efforts to " make his calling and election sure."[2] For that purpose a brief summary of the main features of an act of self-examination may be helpful as representing his first duty, namely, that of seeing to his own soul before venturing to deal with the souls of others. Such a form of self-questioning may proceed somewhat as follows :—

Is my life really and truly dedicated to God's service, given up to the guidance of His Spirit, actuated by the love of His Son as its dominant principle ? If this be the case, I am necessarily in a state of salvation in its twofold sense ; that is to say, I am in a state of deliverance (if not wholly, at all events in a certain real sense and degree) from the bondage of sin, first as to its guilt, and secondly as to its power.

(1) *The Guilt of Sin.*—Am I in a position to assure myself that the sin of my life past—so far as my utmost efforts can enable me to realise and sum it up—has been brought to Jesus Christ, has been repented of, forsaken, and submitted to be cleansed away in His Blood, the continual presentment of which (or the act of death it represents) is the means whereby reconciliation is made for me with His Father from Whose love that sin had separated me ? Have I accepted that reconciliation by an act of faith on my own part, relying upon the Father's promised acceptance of the atonement through the mediation of His Son ?

(2) *The Power of Sin.*—Have I been enabled through the grace of the Holy Spirit to battle against, and in an advancing degree to overcome and to keep under,

---

[1] Song of Songs i. 6.   [2] 2 St. Pet. i. 10.

those sinful influences by which my life in its natural
condition would be actuated ; and am I now faithfully and diligently carrying on the conflict against
those influences, and, notwithstanding many shortcomings, succeeding on the whole ?

Salvation is a negative word ; it represents the
negative side of Christianity, that is, the side which
has relation to the annulling of sin, its influences,
its effects. Hence it only represents one aspect of
the Christian life, namely, that which is concerned with
sin in its effect as the means of separation from the love
of God, the condition which is the starting-point of
man's natural life, and which, in the deepest and fullest
sense of the term, is one of Death. Salvation consists
simply in the removal of this bar of separation, and
is the process of restoring man to a condition of, and
capacity for, the possession of the Divine love.

Our inquiry proceeds now to the *positive* aspect of
the spiritual life, in some such form as the following :—

(1) Have I taken as the ruling motive of my life
the object of seeking and carrying out God's will at
all costs, and at any sacrifice ? Am I daily presenting
my body, " a living sacrifice," striving to make it
" holy, acceptable " unto Him ? [1]

(2) Do I love God with all my heart and soul and
strength ? Or if not so much as this, do I at all events
love Him, and is it my great desire and effort to love
Him more ?

(3) Am I " working out my own salvation with
fear and trembling " ? [2] that is to say, building up my
spiritual life by those means which God has appointed
in His Church, and especially by the regular and
effective participation of the Body and Blood of Christ

---

[1] Rom. xii. 1.   [2] Phil. ii. 12.

in the Sacrament of the Holy Communion, and in those various subsidiary means upon the due observance of which this effective participation in great measure depends ?

(4) Have I deeply at heart, and bound up with my dearest life interests, the welfare of others—temporal and spiritual—and especially of those who are in any sense committed to my charge ?

Even the faithful and diligent priest is in danger of neglecting the care of his own soul while earnestly labouring for the souls of others, and thus imperilling the shipwreck of both interests so far as his own part in them is concerned. It must, therefore, be his daily care to acquire and maintain in his own person the disposition and character which it is the declared aim of his life to cultivate in others. This can only be brought about, on the one hand, by constant union with his Lord ; on the other, by watchfulness for the principles and motives which govern his own conduct. Otherwise, there is danger of his work becoming mechanical, perfunctory, lifeless, unconsecrated, and, hence, devoid of the character of service. This is surely a melancholy condition of things.

The practice of private devotion is, of course, the only fuel which can maintain the fire of the Divine Life in the soul, and can thus cause its outcome in the form of external activity to be an offering acceptable to our Lord and Master. The young minister must keep his own vineyard in due order, cultivated, watered, weeded, pruned, and fruit-bearing, if he would be a fit keeper of other vineyards. It is not enough that the results of a man's labour should be good and beneficial in themselves. This is the case with all action—on the part of evil men as well as of faithful labourers—so far as regards its ultimate results. Our Heavenly Father's disposal of events causes all things to work together for good,[1] whatever may be the motives which actuated the production of each particular event. But the workers are judged, not by the results which follow their work, but by the motive which actuated it. Hence, the result which amounts to failure, so far as appearances go, following upon any course of action, may be as fully productive of rich blessing to the worker as though his efforts had been crowned by the most evident success. It is by the motive of love as an energetic principle—the love which is fostered by close communion with his Lord—that the blessedness of the worker is measured.

If the priest's attention is distracted by multifarious duties which appear as though they could not be neglected without serious detriment—and hence he is tempted to cut short his period for private devotion —let him remember that the accomplishment of God's work which he is endeavouring to effect will be brought about anyhow ; by some other instrument if not by himself : but that the nurture of his own soul can only be accomplished by his own exertion. After all, a man's first duty is that of working out his own salvation. The mistake lies in setting this object (his own personal gain or advantage) before him as a leading motive of action, in keeping this object in view as the ultimate purpose to be attained by his efforts on behalf of others, in forgetting that his main thought is to be for others, not for himself. Herein lies the difference between Christianity and Buddhism, with all the beautiful and Christ-like grace of self-abnegation

[1] *Cp.* Rom. viii. 28.

and altruistic self-sacrifice which the latter system so eminently exhibits. The Buddhist practises the denial of selfish propensities, the performance of good offices towards his fellow-creatures, with a view of promoting his own attainment of Nirvana, or freedom from the domination of passion and sensation. In other words, with an ultimate view to his own self-interest. Christianity teaches the denial of self—practised simply as an offering of love to a loving Lord—the practice of doing good to others from the motive, pure and simple, of love to them, and the desire to promote their welfare without the ulterior motive of gaining blessing and benefit to one's self thereby. This is, at all events, the ideal principle which the position of the follower of Jesus Christ demands as the motive of conduct, even though it be not carried out with absolute perfection. Man works out his own salvation by going out of himself, by throwing forth his affections and interest, first towards his Lord, and secondly, towards his fellows for his Lord's sake. In the very first place, therefore, he is bound to take measures for maintaining unbroken, and ever on the increase, his own condition of close and active communion with his Master in all departments of his life. And this will call for active effort. Prayer is no mere routine duty, but the actual putting forth of spiritual power ; for this to be accomplished effectively it is necessary that in that department of his life, perhaps more than in any other department, the Christian minister's work should be done systematically. The framing of his devotions must occupy a most important place in the apportionment of his life-work.

One essential point to made sure of is that the amount is sufficient—the amount of time bestowed, the amount of spiritual and intellectual activity exerted.

Another important requisite is that the range of subjects included within these devotions be sufficiently comprehensive to include the various departments of worship, which may be roughly stated as seven in number, namely :—

1. Confession and absolution.
2. Praise.
3. Thanksgiving.
4. Self-oblation.
5. Supplication for things needful.
6. Deprecation from evil in its various shapes.
7. Intercession.

The use of manuals may be all very well, but when it comes to the choice of a manual I think it will be a matter of difficulty to find any one among the many in existence which will really supply what is needed in this department. It would be much better that the priest should frame his own system, including all the various forms of need of which he is conscious, and putting it into such shape as best suits his own judgment. This should be done in writing, written and rewritten, with additions, modifications, and alterations such as are suggested from time to time in the course of the regular use of the forms thus drawn up.

The subject of public worship does not fall within the range of our present consideration. Its place in the priestly life is, of course, a matter of the utmost importance, but it may not be treated as in any sense a substitute for private devotion.

One point which needs to be ever kept in mind is the fact that prayer, to be really effectual, must be specific in its character. The worshipper must have clearly in mind the nature of the gifts of which his conscience teaches him the need, and must learn to seek their supply definitely and categorically. Vagueness and lack of particularity are oftentimes the cause as well of deficiency in vigour, as also—consequently—of absence of effect in prayer. " We have not because we ask not." [1] Hence, the worshipper cannot afford to depend on mere general expressions in offering his petitions at the throne of grace. The priest should learn, not only by self-examination, but also by keeping an outlook on the requirements of his position at all points, to include in his regular devotions every form of need, every subject for thanksgiving or praise which belongs to his daily life as an individual and as a minister of the Gospel of Jesus Christ. He should leave no loophole for the entrance of evil unguarded, no form of blessing unremembered, no kind of need unthought of.

I have urged that the priest should plan out his own system of private devotion, and should have it in writing, in such form as to suit his own requirements, instead of depending upon manuals which are the work of others. It has occurred to me, however, that it might possibly be helpful to some of my younger brethren were I to suggest for their consideration a specimen of such a scheme as I here recommend, in the shape which it has taken in the course of years in my own case. An outline of this kind will, therefore, be found as an Appendix, on p. 40.

[1] St. Jas. iv. 2,

PRAYER IN GENERAL

PRAYER is to be regarded not only as a means of effectual approach to our Father's presence, and of rendering service, but also as an *instrument* capable of attaining *definite results*. As such it is imperatively necessary that we should learn to use it ourselves, and also to teach others to use it, for the capacity for turning to account this means of grace will not come of itself. Its acquisition demands careful study and diligent practice. The constituent elements of prayer may be stated as follows :—

(1) Confession and absolution, (2) Thanksgiving, (3) Self-oblation, (4) Praise, (5) Supplication for supply of needs, (6) Deprecation from evil, (7) Intercession. Its forms and methods are, of course, varied according to the character of the various occasions for which it is used. They may be roughly expressed as follows :—

1. Stated daily prayer ; twice or oftener, and certainly not less than three times a day for clergymen and candidates for Holy Orders.

2. Special or occasional prayers ; in any of the above-mentioned forms, arising from any special needs, or from a call for any special object.

3. Ejaculatory or unpremeditated prayers ; the result of momentary thought as in the cases of Nehemiah [1] and Jacob.[2]

[1] Neh. ii. 4 ; perhaps xiii. 14, 22b, 31.   [2] Gen. xxxii. 9.

4. Meditation. (See special section dealing with this practice.)

With regard to the allotment of periods for prayer, it is not my purpose to suggest any rules. These are best arranged by each man for himself, to fit into the plan of his daily duties. I would remark, however, that, in my view, the late evening is the least favourable time for prayer considered as active mental and spiritual effort. At the end of the work day (and for him every day is more or less a day of work) the priest ought to be too tired to be in a condition for giving his best energies to any such effort. The condition of mental activity and excitement of which the priest is often conscious at the close of Sunday, or any other day of unusual mental strain, is something abnormal, and indicative rather of an inflammatory condition than one of healthful vigour. What is needed at such times is rest, not work. The inclination towards the latter which is often present under these circumstances should, therefore, be restrained in the interests of health. The prayers used immediately before retiring for the night should be brief and comprehensive, otherwise they are apt to be looked forward to as a task. This is fatal. Note that the earlier in the day the hour chosen for devotion, the better for its life and effectiveness, and the better you will enjoy it. For although the pleasure to be derived from the practice of prayer and praise may not be regarded as a suitable motive for such actions, or as an object to be sought for its own sake ; and although, again, much effectual prayer is doubtless offered under circumstances which render such offering a matter of almost painful effort, where any sense of pleasure is entirely absent—yet there can be no doubt that where prayer is a reality its observance cannot but be accompanied with much of spiritual enjoyment. This is especially the case with reference to that department of worship which is known as Meditation. In fact, the reality of prayer as such may often be tested by its presence or absence, though it should be remarked that one great reason for the absence of sensible pleasure in the practice of prayer is that of the brevity of our ordinary acts of private worship. To be productive of spiritual enjoyment the act of prayer must be leisurely, so that the mind may dwell on each point as it comes up, and fully grasp its significance. Prayer, to produce a sensation of pleasure, need not be extemporaneous ; the devout utterance of a psalm, with the soul fully alive to the poetry as well as to the inner significance, will often have the effect of an elevation of soul amounting almost to rapture. There can be no doubt that private prayers, as usually practised, are too hurried, although without the least consciousness that such is the case. The question may be asked : " How can time be found for such prolongation of the act of private worship as is here contemplated ? " I would answer this by two suggestions, both of which I have found most effectual in the course of a very busy life.

The first is that of the *utilisation of odds and ends of time*. We see the Roman clergy saying their Office as they sit in the railway carriage, hereby setting us an excellent example. Why should we not utilise the time occupied in our walks and drives, and even that which is spent in waiting for the train at the railway station ? Of course, the objection will at once be raised of the distracting effect of external objects under such circumstances. The answer will be expressed in the second suggestion to which I refer, namely, that of *acquiring the habit of concentration of mind*. Until this habit has been acquired no doubt the difficulty referred to will appear insuperable ; but I can, from my own experience, bear testimony to the fact that the habit of deliberately concentrating the mind upon any subject which may seem desirable may be acquired by patience and perseverance, so as to be effective under almost any ordinary circumstances that can be mentioned. The priest, therefore, should make the acquisition of the power to do this a definite object of effort, and should persevere until he has acquired it. Some men may attain their object more quickly than others, but there is no question that every man is capable of attaining it if he only gives sufficient time and degree of attention to the matter.

It will, in fact, be found, I think in all cases, that the exercise of devotional thought, prayer, and meditation is carried on more effectively, and with greater satisfaction to the worshipper, while walking—whether to and fro in a church or other building, or continuously in the open air—than in any other bodily position or attitude. I have, myself, found that when engaged in the exercise of meditation (or even ordinary prayer) in the attitude of kneeling, any new access from any cause of earnestness or fervour would invariably be accompanied by the impulse to rise and walk to and fro ; and that the exercise resumed in this condition of movement would be carried on more effectively than in the attitude of kneeling or any other stationary position. Nothing is more conducive to spiritual activity, or to life in the practice of devotion, than a walk in the woods, or some quiet spot, where the worshipper feels his capacity for devotional activity enhanced by the companionship of nature.

EVENSONG IN THE WOODS.[1]

" Hush, let us say ' Our Father,' in this wood,
 And through bare boughs look up into the sky,
 Where fleecy clouds on autumn winds go by.
Here, by this fallen trunk, which long since stood
And praised the Lord and Giver of all good,
 We'll sing ' Magnificat.' With curious eye,
 A squirrel watches from a branch on high,
As though he, too, would join us if he could.

" Now in our ' Nunc Dimittis,' soft and low,
 Strange woodland voices mingle, one by one ;
 Dead songs of vanished birds, the sad increase
Of crumpled leaves on paths where rough winds go,
 The deepening shades, the low October sun—
 ' Lord, let Thy servant now depart in peace.' "

Another consideration which may be noticed as
helping to meet the difficulty in respect of the time
occupied by prolonged devotional exercises may be
thus expressed. It will be found that the habit of
mental concentration, the cultivation of which has
been so strongly recommended, will have the effect
of stimulating the capacity for thought in such a way
as to enable the worshipper to follow out intelligently
any train of thought or spiritual action with a rapidity
which, before making the matter a subject of study,
would be thought incredible. I have already referred
to the injurious effect of hurrying our devotions, this
being certainly one of the most serious of the dangers
to be guarded against. But the term " hurrying "
implies the lack of due and full consideration of the
matter which is being dealt with. The persevering
practitioner of the method here under consideration
will find that there is such a thing as rapidity of thought
without hurrying. The latter evil may be avoided if
you make a practice of keeping in mind the necessity

---

[1] "Poems," by Frederick George Scott (Constable & Co., 1910).

for concentration of thought throughout the whole period of the devotional exercises. The *effort* to do this will soon become unnecessary, as it will be found that when once the mind has been definitely made up to the maintenance of this habit of concentration it will soon work itself automatically ; to the effect that as soon as the thoughts begin to drift into another channel, the mind will recognise the fact instinctively, and bring the train of wandering thought to a stop. Wandering thoughts are the great trouble in every form of devotion, and the tendency to them will never, I suppose, be wholly overcome. Yet it may be kept in great measure under control by simply making it a habit to stop short as soon as the drifting tendency is recognised, and to continue the act of devotion with renewed life. The rapidity with which thought can travel, while still maintaining a full grasp of the subject with which it is engaged, is certainly wonderful ; and the acquisition of the capacity for this concentrated and rapid thought will, as has been remarked, form to a considerable extent the solution of the difficulty comprised in the amount of time necessarily occupied by effective private devotion.

Yet, with all this, it is certain that for the due performance of this duty, especially in the case of the priest, a considerable portion of time must necessarily be assigned to it. I suppose it will be universally admitted that the very sinews of spiritual war may be said to consist of prayer. Hence the cutting down of the period spent in prayer, for the sake of the claims of active work, below the limit of time which is really necessary for its effectual observance, will certainly be fatal to the satisfactory performance of that work, as well as most injurious to the spiritual life of the worker ; and the apparent necessity for such cutting down will certainly vanish if only the practice of due economy of time be intelligently followed out. The amount of effective and energetic worship which may, by such measures, be compressed within the limits of, say, two hours per day, would certainly surprise the man who has never systematically set about the work of making his devotion—in method as well as matter—a thing of definite system.

The duty of observing the practice of definite system must surely be recognised as almost the first requisite for the successful fulfilment of the course of duty which belongs to the priestly office. In other walks of life this duty is generally to a great extent forced upon a man ; he has certain objects before him, the accomplishment of which is made absolutely necessary, and the systematic allotment of his time so as to ensure their successful performance is either arranged for him by those who have the direction of his work, or is demanded from him by the necessity of the case. While he is a curate this may be to a great extent the case with the young clergyman, and the multifarious requirements of a town parish may have a similar effect ; [1] but the country clergyman, in the great majority of cases, has no such check upon the economical employment of his time. His duties, apart from the merest official routine, are of his own devising and arrangement. His time is almost wholly at his own disposal, and it is usually possible for him to go through a course of occupation which may seem to himself, and to others, to represent fully the due employment of his time, when, as a matter of fact, the strict observance of definite system would

---

[1] But this is by no means always the case.

make it plain that the amount of time expended was altogether disproportionate to the amount of work done within its limits. I am writing from my own experience as a parish priest. I know what it is for a man to be, if I may so say, *busily idle*, and to have his time apparently full up, whereas the amount of work which is done within a certain period might easily have been compressed within a small fragment of it. I have already spoken of the importance of utilising odds and ends of time, especially that which is spent in travelling, driving, or walking. The time has been when, from the multiplicity of affairs in which I happened to be engaged, it became absolutely necessary for me to turn to such account all periods of this sort, including even the use of the time spent in waiting for the fulfilment of an engagement by some defaulter in this respect. It was by such experience as this that I became aware of the vast importance of economy in the use of time, and of system, as the only method of securing such economy. No doubt the best and most effective means of learning is that of a consideration of one's own mistakes, and most of the suggestions which I am offering for the consideration of my brethren in this present little work have this as their foundation.

Of course, the practice of private devotion, which is all that we have in view in this treatise, should be suitably distributed over the day's course. Each individual clergyman no doubt is the best judge of the method to be observed in his own case. It should be remarked, however, that the period say of fifteen or, perhaps, twenty minutes immediately preceding the midday meal—and thus easily borne in mind and set apart for the purpose—naturally occupies a very important place in the day's devotional system. Our manuals of devotion assign certain subjects for the period of Sext, with which the period we are now considering may roughly correspond. But, however this may be, it is surely manifest that this little period, dividing the day, as it were, into halves, should be turned to account by a brief act of retrospect which recalls to the mind the manner in which the day's first half has been spent, and of prospect, seeking grace and guidance for the due use of that portion which still remains.

FASTING

THE exercise of fasting serves other purposes than that of spiritual discipline. When observed judiciously in moderation, and not followed by the reaction of over-eating, it forms a change which is by all physicians recognised as beneficial to the general health. If there be cases in which the practice has been found injurious this is generally owing either to its being overdone, whether as regards length of time or degree of abstinence, or, on the other hand, to lack of judgment in its method, *e.g.* when prolonged abstinence is accompanied by active exercise or other form of physical strain.

Fasting gives a man clearness of brain and suitableness of frame for mental or spiritual activity, and more especially for such exercises as meditation and prayer. In order that prayer may be offered to the best effect, the mind should be in its freshest and most vigorous condition, and to this condition fasting, when properly conducted, is distinctively helpful.

You sometimes hear the remark made : " I have tried fasting and find that its effect is only that of making me sleepy and stupid and unfit for any real spiritual effort." Such an assertion embodies a sad admission, namely, that the speaker has never yet set himself to give a fair trial to this most important religious exercise. It is certainly true that fasting, when taken up as an occasional or sporadic action, usually carries with it the effect just described. Undertaken in this manner the practice may be rather a hindrance than a help to spiritual life ; may be productive of irritability and peevishness, and disinclination for any sort of effort. It is a duty which can be successively and beneficially observed only after suitable training both of mind and of body. The man must not attempt too much at first, nor should he allow himself to be discouraged by failure in his earlier efforts. The body needs to be trained by gradual deprivation of ordinary nourishment to the extent of bringing about a feeling, not of hungry craving, but rather of indifference to animal appetite, a state of physical quiescence as it were. The stage of hunger and sleepiness will in any case—if the abstinence be prolonged—probably be followed by a condition such as this.

The following form of experience is probably a common one. At the ordinary hour for meals the appetite will usually assert itself, and a certain measure of self-control will be requisite in order to subdue the tendencies towards apathy and irritability. When that time has passed these sensations will, of their own accord, subside, and the body will return to its state of quiescence and the mind to its condition of capability for devotional activity. In referring to my own experience I am not limiting the subject to its devotional aspect. On one occasion while on a canoe expedition in the wilds north of the St. Lawrence, we had fallen short of provisions, and it became necessary to limit our meals to two during the day, that is to say, a morning and an evening meal. The important place taken by each meal in the strenuous life which a journey of this sort implies is familiar to all who have taken part in such life. On the first day of such abstinence, when the time for the ordinary midday meal arrived I was overcome by a sense of utter exhaustion, and the labour of doing my part in the work of paddling seemed almost too much for my powers of endurance. I was naturally filled with consternation, wondering how I should hold out during the privations which lay before us if I broke down at the outset. But I was happily reassured when, the meal hour having passed, I felt my strength returning, and the sense of inner emptiness and exhaustion having passed away, I was able to continue my portion of the day's work without serious discomfort.

The body having been reduced to the state of quiescence just referred to, a condition follows which as regards sensation (or rather diminution of sensation) may in some measure remind us of the progress towards Nirvana which is the aim of the Buddhist's life.[1] The mind is set at liberty to carry on its exercises unimpeded. No doubt some of the most pleasurable forms of sensation of which life is capable are to be found in the practice of contemplation when the mind exercises itself under the influence of fasting, when it is practically untrammelled by the feelings of the body.

One leading aim in the practice of fasting is that of bringing the bodily, as well as the spiritual, system into harmony with the character of God. So far its

[1] The Buddhist's idea is that the cause of evil is sensation, be it of pleasure or pain. The idea of happiness is that of abolition of sensation. So a man by training brings himself to a condition in which he is no longer conscious either of pleasure or pain. This is attained by self-denial, living on the simplest kind of diet, and at the same time overcoming the tendency to self-indulgence and self-seeking by seeking to benefit others. His aim is that of subduing in himself anything which tends to produce pleasure or pain.

resemblance to Buddhism holds good. The difference between Buddhism and Christianity consists in the further motive, which is really the highest and the principal motive, namely, that of simple love for God, and the giving forth of the soul to Him in the use of means which are calculated to promote the approach thus aimed at. The desire for nearness to God, and the capacity for doing His will because He wills it, apart from the ulterior desire to acquire benefit, whether spiritual or otherwise, for one's self, this is the motive which stands alone as the noblest and the highest of which creature life is capable. In Buddhism the motive for self-denial is simply that of self-development, self-improvement ; in Christianity it is that of love only ; love first towards God, and secondly, towards mankind for God's sake, as being made in God's image. This is, then, the great motive to be aimed at in the practice of fasting, as in all other religious exercises.

As we have already seen, the effects of fasting on the intellect, even as a mere physical exercise, are decidedly beneficial. Those who have given the practice a fair trial will certainly bear witness to the wonderful clearness of brain, as well as the sense of inward calm and superiority to incidental cares, which is the natural consequence of the bodily con-dition thus induced. This is accompanied by a sense of mental vigour and capacity for spiritual thought. Fasting, almost of itself, has a purifying effect on the mind and an elevating effect on the spirit. One reason for this probably lies in the physical fact that the energies are not being absorbed in the work of digestion.

Of course, the thing may be overdone, and it is, therefore, necessary to regulate this practice carefully

C

in accordance with its evident operation on body, mind, and spirit. The Christian's duty, undoubtedly, includes the nurture of his body as the instrument given him for working out the glory of God, the well-being of man, and his own salvation. The charge of this instrument calls for his most careful attention in order to keep it in full and effective working order; this is to be borne in mind as an aim to be kept in view, although subordinate to the higher motive of pure, unselfish love towards God. A remembrance of the object which he has in view in so doing will guard him against anything like indulging or pampering the body as such. At the same time it may be observed that the practice followed by many saintly persons— although, perhaps, seldom to any serious extent in these present days—of macerating and enfeebling the body by an undue and exaggerated observance of the exercise of fasting, is clearly a contravention of the purpose, just considered, for which the body was given us, namely, to be made the temple of the Holy Ghost, and an instrument for the active promotion of the glory of God.

It is, therefore, an unquestionable duty to keep the body in a state of fitness and readiness, fully equipped at all points, for the fulfilment of this object. " Mens sana in corpore sano " must be the priest's maxim as regards his attention to his own personality in its mental and physical aspects.

FASTING COMMUNION

THIS expression is, strictly speaking, a misnomer, since what is signified by it does not
necessarily imply the practice of fasting considered in
its true sense of deprivation of ordinary food. When
the Communion is made, as is usually the case, early
in the morning, there is no question of fasting in the
true sense of the term. It would be better, therefore,
that the practice should be designated by some other
term.

With regard to the practice itself, no doubt the
leading principle upon which it is founded is a good
one, whether considered as implying the idea of reverence, or that of fitness for the Sacrament in the sense
of mental and spiritual receptivity. This principle
appears to require that on the ground of reverence
it is manifestly proper that provision should be made
for a due vacancy in the physical frame for the reception
of the sacred Body and Blood. Further ground
on which the practice would seem desirable is that
of the suitable mental frame thus induced, the faculties
being certainly clearer and more vigorous when a certain interval has elapsed after a full meal. Again,
the spiritual condition thus promoted, of calm, quiet,
and self-control, is always to be considered. So far,
then, as the practice implies the interposition of an
interval sufficient for reverent reception as well as for

mental and spiritual fitness for the apprehension of
the benefit, the practice would appear to be not only
right and seemly, but actually called for by the needs
of the case.

The question next arises by what rule the interposition of this period or interval is to be regulated.
The prevailing view is to the effect that the starting
point of the abstinence should necessarily be not later
than the hour of midnight, whatever may be the hour of
the day following at which the Communion is made.
This view of the case is, of course, very widely followed,
and has been the rule from a very early period.   But it
may be questioned whether it has not acted to a certain
extent as an obstacle to the very practice which it is
designed to enforce.   If we bear in mind simply the
twofold object which the practice would appear mainly
intended to promote, the question would arise whether
its due observance does not depend rather upon the
nature and length of the interval between the act of
Communion and the last preceding meal, than on the
assignment of any particular period from which the
time of abstinence is to be reckoned.

For example, supposing one man should take a
late supper and communicate very early the next
morning, say five or six o'clock ; and that another
man should take an early breakfast, say at seven or
half-past seven, and that in his case the act of Communion were to be about midday (probably after that
time if the Communion were a choral one), the physical
effect, as regards bodily preparedness, would most
likely be more effectual in the latter case than in the
former, as the process of digestion proceeds much more
rapidly during waking hours than during hours of
sleep.

This suggestion would no doubt be met on the part of many with indignant dissent.[1] The view that it is seemly that the Sacrament should be the first food entering the system on the day of Communion is certainly worthy of full consideration, but, after all, is a matter of sentiment only. And it is a question whether it is a sufficient reason for making the practice of so-called " Fasting Communion " a hard-and-fast rule to which no exception shall be allowed. Surely the first point to be considered in dealing with such a question is that of the due preparedness of the system for the reverent and effective use of the Sacrament. Obviously, this condition of due preparedness cannot be said to exist during the process of digestion immediately following a full meal ; nor on the other hand, can such a state of reverent fitness be predicated when abstinence from food has been prolonged to the extent of producing a disordered state of the digestive organs. The long period of abstinence involved in the usual practice of abstaining from food from the night of the previous day until after noon on the day of the celebration must, in most cases, be felt as a tax upon the physical energies. This is evidenced by the fact that some priests endeavour to meet it in some degree by lying late in bed, a practice most surely to be deprecated. Even when this is not the case, prolonged fasting under circumstances of active movement and expenditure is generally followed by a somewhat disordered state of the digestive organs, productive of a condition the reverse of that which reverence would seek to ensure as suitable for the solemn repast we are

[1] This view has been criticised as objectionable. But is it not an unquestionable fact that physical conditions in the hygienic sense have a distinct effect, advantageous or disadvantageous, on spiritual exercise in its various forms ?

considering. Surely the question is not one of hours of the day, but of the effect to be produced ; and whatever may best conduce, even in a physical sense, to a suitable effect is necessarily the first point to be aimed at, even though it may involve the departure from stereotyped rules.

MEDITATION

MEDITATION may be regarded as in a sense the highest form of private devotion ; perhaps, also, the most difficult. It demands, and implies, a condition of actual nearness to the life of Christ, as well as direct and effectual consciousness of His Presence. The practice of this form of devotion is, perhaps, one of the surest means of testing the reality of one's spiritual life. It may be said with truth that there can be no *live* Christianity without the existence of this practice in greater or less degree. No diligence in other forms of devotion can make up for the want of this one. It is in itself necessarily extemporaneous. Stated prayers naturally crystallise into fixed forms of words, and no doubt it is best that this should be so ; the exercise of prayer may even gain in force and intensity by the use of this method of worship, the use, that is, of forms probably of one's own composition and stereotyped by continual practice : the effort to use varying language often distracts the mind from the substance of the object sought for. Meditation, however, is necessarily extemporaneous, and the idea of its nature is probably best arrived at by consulting the models of meditation which the Church has given to us in her earliest and simplest years. The typical instance which at once rises to our minds is that model of this species of composition,

St. Augustine's Confessions—a work which for nearly a millennium and a half has stirred the hearts of multitudes as, perhaps, no other work, outside the Scriptures, has ever done.[1] St. Ambrose, St. Anselm, as well as *The Imitation of Christ* (in its meditative portions) are also models of this form of exercise. The study of these works will provide a plain answer to the question : " In what does meditation, considered as a religious act, consist ? " It may be defined as a dialogue between the soul and its Lord. Herein consists its difference from a mere act of reflection ; in the fact, namely, that there are always two persons engaged in it. Hence, in the models to which reference has been made, meditation always takes the shape of direct address to God : " Magnus es Domine et laudabilis valde," begins *St. Augustine's Confessions*. A dialogue means a conversation between two, and the dialogue in this case consists in the fact, which every really successful effort at this form of exercise will bring about, that the man who habituates himself in this manner to address his inmost thoughts directly to God, will soon discover that the very act of so doing has the effect of introducing into his mind, as responses to his own utterances, thoughts which are certainly not originated there ; thoughts deeper and higher than any of which he would be capable by his own personal mental efforts. It is not that anything in the shape of direct and consciously recognised response is to be expected. The worshipper is addressing to God, as they occur to his mind, what would appear to himself to be his own thoughts. He will find, however, that these thoughts, as they shape themselves in his

---

[1] Compare St. Paul and St. John, on the one hand, with St. Augustine and Thomas à Kempis on the other.

mind and find expression in words, are by degrees coming to be the expression of new ideas which are certainly not his own, of deeper purport than his own unaided mind could have conceived of itself. He will be conscious of a certain sense of inspiration, his soul kindled with a sense of nearness to his Lord, and personal contact with His Presence.

It will generally be found most natural to address your meditation to the Lord Jesus, His humanity being your point of contact with the Godhead, His humanity being wholly sympathetic with your humanity. In some cases, perhaps, it may be found more helpful to address the utterances directly to the Father, ever bearing in mind and leaning upon the mediation of the Son. An essential to meditation is the remembrance of the fact that there are two parties to it. The soul in addressing itself to its Lord does so in the distinct *expectation* of a response on His part which will, as it were, convey itself to the man's mind through the medium of the mind's own current of thought. It is this view of the subject which affords the key to the effective performance of this form of worship.

Now comes the question of how to conduct it. As a practical observance this form of exercise has been much hindered by making it a subject of rules and regulations such as those which are laid down in ordinary manuals. To enjoy the full advantage of the exercise the worshipper should be advised to keep clear of manuals. Avoid formality. Do away with the physical tedium which naturally attends perseverance in any single attitude for any length of time, as this certainly detracts from the *life* of the exercise. The attitude of kneeling is generally not desirable, and it is worth while remembering that ambulatories and cloisters were constructed with the object of affording opportunity for ambulatory prayer. Walking to and fro in church or chapel, or in a quiet spot out of doors, will generally be found most conducive to the exercise of meditation. Outside, indeed, the objects of external nature will generally become a help rather than a hindrance to the exercise of meditation, assisting the worshipper to recognise and appropriate as his own that Real Presence which pervades the universe.[1]

In the practice of meditation two difficulties may be mentioned which naturally present themselves : (1) the difficulty of attaining anything like a distinct realisation of the presence of our Lord ; (2) that of giving definite and practical shape to the exercise of meditation, and so making it really profitable. The first difficulty will soon yield to earnest endeavour. You have only to make the Presence a reality to yourself by treating it as a real thing, even though you may not at once attain that fuller sense of reality which is the object you are striving after, and which will come in due time. Even though this sense of conscious perception of the Divine Presence should be slow in making itself clearly manifest, do not worry about it. Though your eyes are for the time holden, it does not follow that your Lord is not truly present with you—as truly present as He was with the travellers on the way to Emmaus, for even they were not certain until almost after the event—present, listening to you and even answering you through the medium of your own thoughts, even as He directed the current of the thoughts of Cleopas and his companion.[2] The great

[1] See notes on Divine Immanence appended to Scheme of Prayer, p. 51 ff.
[2] St. Luke xxiv. 13-35.

secret of success is that of treating Him as actually present, only making sure that you are genuinely striving towards the realisation of that actual Presence, and not allowing yourself to be disturbed either by failure in realising it or by absence of fervour or warmth of feeling at first.

The second difficulty, that of giving practical shape to the meditation itself, calls for careful consideration, and must be explicitly dealt with. Meditation to be of any use must be a practical thing ; mere devout dreaming is not the thing you are aiming at. The practice of this exercise with any degree of real benefit is no light or easy matter. It calls for steady and strenuous effort. Much depends upon the selection of your subject ; this must be something clear and definite, something which you feel to be essential to your soul's requirements. It may be a particular form of need, of difficulty, of sin, of infirmity, of sorrow, of perplexity, of anxiety, of joy or comfort, of thankfulness or praise—some thought or question calling for an expression on your part, and seeking an answer on the part of your Lord.

A text of Scripture may oftentimes be selected as a starting point, and it is desirable to supply yourself with material for following up any thoughts which may occur. The Bible and Greek Testament will be essential, and a small Greek Testament Concordance will also be very helpful. It is very necessary to have a distinct and practical purpose before you, something definite to be kept in view, or there is a danger of degenerating into devout dreaming. You must take heed that your subject follows a definite line of thought, and does not diverge into by-paths. To avoid this latter you will need to preserve your recollectedness, your consciousness of the presence of Him Whom you are addressing, as well as the attitude of attention, as *expecting, looking for, a response from Him,* to be borne in upon your mind in the form of luminous and elevating thoughts.

This practice of meditation will be found to acquire a character of fascination belonging to no other form of mental or spiritual exercise. The worshipper will be surprised by the manner in which, apparently by the sole process of his own thoughts, difficulties will clear themselves away, while doubt and uncertainty, trouble and despondency, and mental disquiet, will give place to a sense of peace and comfort, and even joy. But in order that this happy result may follow it is necessary that plenty of time should be allowed. Anything like haste will be fatal to its profitable observance. It should never be undertaken unless under circumstances which will afford sufficient time for the deliberate expansion of thought in which the essence of this exercise consists.

One very suitable subject for meditation would be that of hindrances to the spiritual life, in those special forms which most beset the worshipper at that particular time. The treatment of these is generally conducive to a sense of comfort, and even joy, which is one of the usual accompaniments of this exercise.

INTERCESSION

THE scheme for the Office of Worship, which is given in the Appendix, does not, it will be observed, include the important feature of intercession. The pastor's devotional system must include a most careful and sufficient arrangement of this form of duty, or his position as a pastor must necessarily be utterly ineffectual. The various objects which call for the exercise of spiritual energy in this respect will have to be carefully arranged and apportioned to their different departments, and the frequency with which each object takes its place in his act of intercession will have to be carefully adapted to its necessities and claims.

One fundamental requisite underlying the whole subject of prayer is that of a clear assurance of objective answer to it. The view of a mere subjective effect on the mind and soul of the worshipper is utterly subversive of any reality in the worship. When we find a man occupying a position which may be called that of an outside thinker—the position of up-to-date scientific thought, as is the case with Sir Oliver Lodge— never finding any difficulty in the idea of an objective answer to prayer, surely the Christian priest must be regarded as woefully falling short of the demands of his position should he allow himself to entertain any doubt on the subject. I only refer to this point because it is unquestionable that such doubts have existed and have found expression even on the part of those who consider themselves Christians. There must be the clear persuasion that all real prayer must have its objective answer, although it may not be in the actual form in which the prayer is expressed, or which the worshipper contemplates. Without this persuasion it will be impossible to exercise the force and fervour in the act of prayer which alone can make it an actual power for bringing about definite results.

The priest's intercession must be carefully planned so as to include all such objects as have a right to claim his assistance in this respect ; the Church at large, the nation (and the various leading cases of need in each, with more special reference to cases which call for special note for the time being) ; missions and missionaries should, of course, have a special place in their due order ; and so with many other objects which may be included in the term *classes*. But, of course, a just proportion of the work of intercession is that which is included within the priest's own special sphere of labour : " the flock, in which the Holy Ghost has placed him as overseer, to tend the Church of God which He acquired by His own blood." [1] Each department of his work of parish organisation must have its proper share in his prayers regularly, and with such proper frequency as each case may seem to call for.

As regards the intercession for individuals, the exercise of much judgment and discretion will be required in the observance of this department of the work. In the first place, it is manifestly impossible that the number of objects included in this form of

[1] Acts xx. 28.

supplication should be unlimited. A certain measure of selection will, therefore, have to be exercised in the choice of those whose names will be included in the list of persons for whom special prayer is to be offered. Those whose claims may seem to be the most imperative are, perhaps, those who themselves would least desire or appreciate the benefits. The erring, the fallen, the negligent, wanderers from the fold, those under pressure of present special need, the sick, the sorrowful, the bereaved, and so forth, will also have their special claims.

One important point I would commend strongly to the consideration of my brethren, namely, that the case of each individual should be distinctly isolated ; that all that is desired on behalf of any person should be asked on his behalf as a separate act ; that is, that one should not pray for individuals in groups, the same petition including a list of names, simply because the needs of all are practically the same. To make prayer a real act of force for the benefit of any individual it would seem that the whole prayer should be offered for him separately, even though it be necessary to repeat the same petition word for word for each of a large number of individuals. I have, in my own case, found this necessary to impart any consciousness of efficiency to prayer considered as an act of power.

Distinction has to be made in the matter of prayer between classes and individuals. Classes are, of course, to be dealt with as such, and each to be dealt with as a unit. If the case of any member of a class calls for separate consideration it will naturally be considered separately.

Objection will probably be raised to the length of time which would be necessitated by the observance of this rule. This difficulty may in great measure be met by the consideration, already referred to,[1] of the acceleration of mental capacity which is the result of cultivation of the habit of mental concentration. The priest will, no doubt, provide himself with a formula including the general range of need applicable to all persons alike, and will simply, by an act of mental apprehension, isolate each case as it comes, and apply to it with energy and vigour the various items of supplication ; his knowledge of the individual imparting the element of freshness and variety to each application of the one form of words.

In the department of intercession the pastor should seek for assistance and co-operation from those members of his flock who are capable of rendering such assistance ; and this would plainly be specially the case with those who are themselves laid aside from active life by sickness or infirmity, and who possess the qualifications of spirituality and devoutness. These lay helpers must be given to understand that a real and definite result is expected by way of answer to their prayers. It may be well to provide them with a definite formula expressing fully the nature of the needs for which their prayers are invited ; though in some cases the priest may feel it sufficient to leave to the helpers themselves the work of putting their petitions into shape. Those whose aid is thus invited are themselves benefited to an incalculable degree, in addition to the value of their services in rendering aid to others. Thus they may be rendered conscious of the significance of those memorable words at the close of Milton's sonnet :

"They also serve, who only stand and wait."

---

[1] Page 15.

In giving directions to those whom you wish to employ in this manner it will be necessary to enlist their interest in order that they may enter heart and soul into the work which they are undertaking. For this purpose it will be desirable to give them such particulars with reference to the case which you are entrusting to their care as may enable them to picture to themselves the object which they are to have in view with sufficient distinctness. It may not be necessary to give them the names of the persons for whom their prayers are asked, but it will be necessary to give them such a sufficient description of the circumstances with reference to which their prayers are needed as will enable them to make their prayers a living reality. Vagueness, dimness, and uncertainty in the object to which attention is directed must necessarily render it practically impossible to regard it with any living interest.

OUTLINE OF SUGGESTED SYSTEM
FOR PRIVATE DEVOTIONS

GRANT, we beseech Thee, merciful Lord, to Thy trustful servants pardon and peace, that they may be cleansed from all their sins, and serve Thee with a quiet mind : through Jesus Christ our Lord. Amen.

> Lord, have mercy upon us.
> Christ, have mercy upon us.
> Lord, have mercy upon us.

Our Father, which art in heaven, Hallowed be Thy Name, Thy kingdom come, Thy will be done in earth, as it is in heaven. Give us this day our daily bread ; And forgive us our trespasses, As we forgive them that trespass against us ; And lead us not into temptation, But deliver us from evil. For Thine is the kingdom, the power, and the glory, For ever and ever. Amen.

Psalm 104

1. Praise the Lord, O my soul : O Lord my God, thou art become exceeding glorious ; thou art clothed with majesty and honour.

2. Thou deckest thyself with light as it were with a garment : and spreadest out the heavens like a curtain.

3. Who layeth the beams of his chambers in the

waters: and maketh the clouds his chariot, and walketh upon the wings of the wind.

4. He maketh his angels spirits: and his ministers a flaming fire.

5. He laid the foundations of the earth: that it never should move at any time.

6. Thou coveredst it with the deep like as with a garment: the waters stand in the hills.

7. At thy rebuke they flee: at the voice of thy thunder they are afraid.

8. They go up as high as the hills, and down to the valleys beneath: even unto the place which thou hast appointed for them.

9. Thou hast set them their bounds which they shall not pass: neither turn again to cover the earth.

10. He sendeth the springs into the rivers: which run among the hills.

11. All beasts of the field drink thereof: and the wild asses quench their thirst.

12. Beside them shall the fowls of the air have their habitation: and sing among the branches.

13. He watereth the hills from above: the earth is filled with the fruit of thy works.

14. He bringeth forth grass for the cattle: and green herb for the service of men.

15. That he may bring food out of the earth, and wine that maketh glad the heart of man: and oil to make him a cheerful countenance, and bread to strengthen man's heart.

16. The trees of the Lord also are full of sap: even the cedars of Libanus which he hath planted;

17. Wherein the birds make their nests: and the fir trees are a dwelling for the stork.

18. The high hills are a refuge for the wild goats: and so are the stony rocks for the conies.

19. He appointed the moon for certain seasons: and the sun knoweth his going down.

20. Thou makest darkness that it may be night : wherein all the beasts of the forest do move.

21. The lions roaring after their prey : do seek their meat from God.

22. The sun ariseth, and they get them away together : and lay them down in their dens.

23. Man goeth forth to his work, and to his labour : until the evening.

24. O Lord, how manifold are thy works : in wisdom hast thou made them all ; the earth is full of thy riches.

25. So is the great and wide sea also : wherein are things creeping innumerable, both small and great beasts.

26. There go the ships, and there is that Leviathan : whom thou hast made to take his pastime therein.

27. These wait all upon thee : that thou mayest give them their meat in due season.

28. When thou givest it them they gather it : and when thou openest thy hand they are filled with good.

29. When thou hidest thy face they are troubled : when thou takest away their breath they die, and are turned again to their dust.

30. When thou lettest thy breath go forth they shall be made : and thou shalt renew the face of the earth.

31. The glorious majesty of the Lord shall endure for ever : the Lord shall rejoice in his works.

32. The earth shall tremble at the look of him : if he do but touch the hills, they shall smoke.

33. I will sing unto the Lord as long as I live : I will praise my God while I have my being.

34. And so shall my words please him : my joy shall be in the Lord.

35. As for sinners, they shall be consumed out of the earth, and the ungodly shall come to an end : praise thou the Lord, O my soul, praise the Lord.

Glory be to the Father, and to the Son : and to the Holy Ghost.

As it was in the beginning, is now, and ever shall be : world without end.   Amen.

Psalm 145

1. I will magnify thee, O God, my King ; and I will praise thy Name for ever and ever.

2. Every day will I give thanks unto thee : and praise thy Name for ever and ever.

3. Great is the Lord, and marvellous worthy to be praised : there is no end of his greatness.

4. One generation shall praise thy works unto another : and declare thy power.

5. As for me, I will be talking of thy worship : thy glory, thy praise, and wondrous works ;

6. So that men shall speak of the might of thy marvellous acts : and I will also tell of thy greatness.

7. The memorial of thine abundant kindness shall be shewed : and men shall sing of thy righteousness.

8. The Lord is gracious and merciful : long-suffering and of great goodness.

9. The Lord is loving unto every man : and his mercy is over all his works.

10. All thy works praise thee, O Lord : and thy saints give thanks unto thee.

11. They shew the glory of thy kingdom : and talk of thy power ;

12. That thy power, thy glory, and mightiness of thy kingdom : might be known unto men.

13. Thy kingdom is an everlasting kingdom : and thy dominion endureth throughout all ages.

14. The Lord upholdeth all such as fall : and lifteth up all those that are down.

15. The eyes of all wait upon thee, O Lord : and thou givest them their meat in due season.

16. Thou openest thine hand : and fillest all things living with plenteousness.

17. The Lord is righteous in all his ways : and holy in all his works.

18. The Lord is nigh unto all them that call upon him : yea, all such as call upon him faithfully.

19. He will fulfil the desire of them that fear him : he also will hear their cry, and will help them.

20. The Lord preserveth all them that love him : but scattereth abroad all the ungodly.

21. My mouth shall speak the praise of the Lord : and let all flesh give thanks unto his holy Name for ever and ever.

Glory be to the Father, and to the Son : and to the Holy Ghost.

As it was in the beginning, is now, and ever shall be : world without end.   Amen.

Glory be to God on high, and in earth peace, goodwill towards men.   We praise Thee, we bless Thee, we worship Thee, we glorify Thee, we give thanks to Thee for Thy great glory, O Lord God, heavenly King, God the Father Almighty.

O Lord, the only-begotten Son Jesu Christ ; O Lord God, Lamb of God, Son of the Father, that takest away the sins of the world, have mercy upon us. Thou that takest away the sins of the world, receive our prayer.   Thou that sittest at the right hand of God the Father, have mercy upon us.

For Thou only art holy ; Thou only art the Lord ; Thou only, O Christ, with the Holy Ghost, art most high in the glory of God the Father.   Amen.

1. Praise the Lord, O my soul : and all that is within me praise his holy Name.

2. Praise the Lord, O my soul ; and forget not all his benefits,

3. Who forgiveth all thy sin : and healeth all thine infirmities :

4. Who saveth thy life from destruction : and crowneth thee with mercy and loving-kindness.

5. The Lord's Name be praised : from the rising up of the sun to the going down thereof.

Glory be to the Father, and to the Son : and to the Holy Ghost.

As it was in the beginning, is now, and ever shall be : world without end. Amen.

PERSONAL THANKSGIVING

Thanks and praise to God for His mercies—eyesight, hearing, reason, activity, and health of body and powers of mind, worldly means and provision for temporal needs, friends, His forbearance and long-suffering, but chiefly for the knowledge of Himself and for eternal life in union with His Son through the Holy Spirit.

SELF-OBLATION

Offer myself to God. Acknowledge that I am unable, unworthy to offer, unfit for His reception. Pray that He will accept, and forgive, and subdue me to His will, that I may be His in body, soul, and spirit.

CONFESSION

I. *My besetting sin*, with careful thought and sorrowful acknowledgment of the various aspects in which it is manifested in the day's life.

II. *Bloodguiltiness.*—(1) Those to whom (by example, influence, direct suggestion offensive to Thee, or failure of duty) I may have in any way been the means of at any time leading into or encouraging in sin, and whose blood cries against me from the ground.

May the precious Blood of Jesus, which speaketh better things than that of Abel, plead for me to Thee and to them ; plead for me and for them ; save me and save them ; and deliver me from blood-guiltiness.

(2) Those whom I have injured by neglect, and whose blood, etc.

May the precious Blood of Jesus, etc.

(3) Those towards whom I may have shown myself untrustworthy, and whose blood, etc.

May the precious Blood of Jesus, etc.

(4) Those whom I have injured by thought, word, and deed ; by doing and leaving undone, and whose blood, etc.

May the precious Blood of Jesus, etc.

III. *Presumption against Thee.*—(1) Let me consider my action in taking upon me this ministry, whether I may not in so doing have been guilty of presumption against Thee.

May the precious Blood of Jesus cleanse me, forgive me, and save me, for Thy mercy's sake.

(2) That I have defiled it by wilful sin.

May the precious Blood of Jesus, etc.

(3) That I have taken Thy Holy Name in vain.

May the precious Blood forgive me, and grant me grace to worship Thee in spirit and in truth.

(4) That I have grieved Thy Holy Spirit.

May the precious Blood of Jesus cleanse me, forgive me, and save me, for Thy mercy's sake.

IV. *My Selfishness and Self-indulgence.*—(1) May the precious Blood cleanse me, forgive me, and grant me grace to take up my cross and follow in the Saviour's steps.

(2) My self-seeking.

May the precious Blood cleanse me, forgive me, and grant me grace to seek Thy glory and the good of Thy Church.

(3) My self-will.

May the precious Blood cleanse me, and grant me grace to bring into captivity every thought to the obedience of Christ.

Grant that I may trust in Thee with all my heart, and lean not to mine own understanding : in all my ways acknowledge Thee ; and do Thou, O Lord, direct my paths.

(4) My self-conceit and pride.

May the precious Blood cleanse me, and grant me grace to abhor myself, and to repent in dust and ashes.

(5) My self-assertiveness and evil temper.

May the precious Blood cleanse me, and grant me grace to be gentle and kind and forbearing.

(6) My timidity and fear of men.

May the precious Blood cleanse me, and grant me grace to be faithful, fearless, and courageous in these respects.

(7) My censoriousness, judgment of others, and uncharitableness.

May the precious Blood cleanse me, and grant me grace to treat others, and think of others, and speak of others, as better than myself.

(8) My unsympathy.

May the precious Blood cleanse me, and grant me grace to be moved with compassion, and to spend and be spent for others.

(9) My impenitence.

May the precious Blood cleanse me, and grant me grace to repent, and confess, and turn from my sins.

(10) My unfaith.

May the precious Blood cleanse me, and grant me grace to embrace and hold fast the blessed hope of everlasting life in our Saviour Jesus Christ.

(11) My ingratitude, and want of love to Thee.

Lord, I am unfit, unworthy to love Thee. May

the Blood of Jesus Christ cleanse me. And may Thy Holy Spirit cleanse the thoughts of my heart that I may perfectly love Thee, and worthily magnify Thy Holy Name.

(12) My unfaithfulness to duty.

May the precious Blood cleanse me, and grant me grace to be as faithful as Moses in all his house.

(13) My untruth.

May the precious Blood cleanse me, and grant me grace to know the truth and to walk in the truth, that the truth may make me free.

May the Blood of Jesus cleanse me from all sin, and deliver me from its power. Though we be tied and bound with the chain of our sins, yet let the pitifulness of Thy great mercy loose us, for the honour of Jesus Christ our Mediator and Advocate.

O Lord, grant me Thy Holy Spirit.

Create in me a clean heart, O God, and renew a right spirit within me.

Cast me not away from Thy presence, and take not Thy Holy Spirit from me.

O give me the comfort of Thy help again, and stablish me with Thy free Spirit.

Grant me light that I may know Thy will.

Grant me fear ; lighten mine eyes that I sleep not in death.

Grant me power ; crush down within me the principle of evil.

O Lord, Thou knowest that the way of man is not in himself : it is not in man that walketh to direct his steps.

O Lord, correct me, but with judgment : not in thine anger, lest Thou bring me to nothing.

Grant me power : work in me to will and to do for Thy good pleasure.

Order my footsteps in Thy word, and so shall no wickedness have dominion over me.

Make me to do the thing that pleaseth Thee, for Thou art my God.

Let Thy good Spirit lead me in the paths of righteousness.

Grant that I may work out my own salvation in fear and trembling.

Strengthen me with might by Thy Holy Spirit in the inner man, that Christ may dwell in my heart by faith.   That I, being rooted and grounded in love, may be able to apprehend with all saints what is the breadth, and length, and depth, and height ; and to know the love of Christ which passeth knowledge : that I may be filled with all the fulness of God.

DEPRECATION

Save me from the devil. Grant that I may resist the devil and that he may flee from me. For I flee unto Thee to hide me.

Save me from my evil heart.   For I flee unto Thee to hide me.

Grant that I may keep my body and bring it into subjection.   For I flee unto Thee to hide me.

Save me from temptation and through temptation. Grant that I may resist and that I may watch and pray that I enter not into temptation. For I flee unto Thee to hide me.

Save me in all my dealings with men. For I flee unto Thee to hide me.

Grant that I may follow peace with all men, and holiness without which no man can see the Lord. For I flee unto Thee to hide me.

Save me from the world's temptation. For I flee unto Thee to hide me.

Hold up my goings in Thy paths. For I flee unto Thee to hide me.

Hear me, O Lord, for Jesus Christ's sake.

GIFTS OF THE SPIRIT

I. Grant that by Thy Holy Spirit's grace my heart may be—
- (1) Awakened.
- (2) Enlightened.
- (3) Moved.
- (4) Subdued.
- (5) Drawn.
- (6) Opened.
- (7) Enkindled.

II. Grant me the spirit of penitence, a broken and a contrite heart, that I may (1) repent, (2) confess, (3) turn from, my sins.

Grant me the spirit of faith that I may embrace and hold fast the blessed hope of eternal life in Christ Jesus.

May the Blood of Jesus cleanse me from all sin.

May I know the love of Christ that passeth knowledge, that I may be filled with all the fulness of God.

III. Save me from a spirit of—
- (1) Self-indulgence.
- (2) Self-seeking.
- (3) Self-conceit.
- (4) Self-will.
- (5) Untruth.
- (6) Uncharity.
- (7) Self-deceiving.

IV. Inspire me with—
- (1) Love for Thee, and a shepherd's love for souls.
- (2) Zeal for Thy glory, and faithful diligence.
- (3) Wisdom, judgment, discretion.
- (4) Self-denial and self-abnegation.
- (5) Faith, courage, and steadfastness.
- (6) Gentleness, meekness, and humility.
- (7) Knowledge :
  - (a) Open my heart that I may seek Thee.

(*b*) Open my eyes that I may see Thee, and see wondrous things out of Thy law.

(*c*) Open my understanding that I may understand the Scriptures.

(*d*) Enlighten my mind that I may know Thee, the only true God, and Jesus Christ Whom Thou hast sent, and in this knowledge find life for my soul.

(*e*) Grant that I may stand in Thy temple and speak to Thy people the words of this life.

(*f*) Purge my lips with a coal from Thine altar. Kindle my lips with a coal from Thine altar. Put Thy word into my lips that it may be as fire, and as the hammer that breaketh rocks in pieces.

(*g*) Open the hearts of Thy people that they may attend to me, and receive with meekness the engrafted word which is able to save their souls.

(*h*) Prosper Thy word in my lips, and Thy work in my hands, that it may be blessed for Thy glory—

    (1) In winning souls.
    (2) In feeding Thy flock.
    (3) In unity.
    (4) In healing.
    (5) In correction.
    (6) In pulling down.
    (7) In building up.

It will be observed that in the foregoing office a conspicuous position has been given to certain selected psalms, and it may not be out of place to offer a few suggestive thoughts on the subject of the devotional use of the Psalms in an aspect which, perhaps, has not received hitherto the attention that, doubtless, will be given to it in the future ; I mean that which sets forth the Immanence of Jehovah throughout the universe in the Person of the Logos.

This glorious truth found expression in the writings of the early Greek Fathers, especially Athanasius, but was lost sight of throughout a large portion of the Church's life. It seems to pass almost out of view during the Middle Ages, and does not reappear in any measure in what may be called the modern systems of religion. Of late years its realisation has been revived (and it will probably take an important place in the attention of the religious world), and there is every prospect of its being restored to its due position in the attention of the religious world in the immediate future. There can be no doubt that the full apprehension of this truth must have the effect of imparting life and interest and gladness to the practice of devotion, such as would hardly be attainable from any other source. It is a truth which is now beginning to find expression on all sides of us.

The part taken by the Logos, first, in the work of creation, and secondly in the act of sustaining and developing the object thus brought into being, is beginning to take its place in the spiritual life, and one result of this consciousness takes shape in a new feeling of admiration for natural scenery in a degree far surpassing what that feeling could be when actuated by any lower consideration. The thought that every object of beauty and order which the senses are capable of perceiving is a presentment of some quality or attribute in the character of God, and—more than this—that it has this quality from the fact of the actual and literal presence of the Divine Logos, which presence imparts to it the character it thus manifests, is one of the most inspiring which the mind is capable of conceiving. As Dr. Liddon says, " He (the Logos) does in a real sense Himself exist in each created object, not as being one with it, but as upholding it in being. He is in every such object the constituting, sustaining, binding force which perpetuates its being." [1] Light-foot, in his Commentary on the Colossians, speaks of the Logos as the sustaining principle which keeps every object in creation in its present condition of cohesion : " He is the principle of cohesion in the universe. He impresses upon creation that unity and solidarity which makes it a cosmos instead of a chaos. Thus, to take one instance, the action of gravitation which keeps in their places things fixed, and regulates the motions of things moving, is an expression of His mind." [2]

This is the vast truth which pantheism gropes after and only fails to reach because it stops short with a half-truth, making its Logos an impersonal principle, immanent, but not transcendent. When once the true view of the Divine Immanence has been distinctly apprehended, and a man realises that the landscape which delights his system of physical sensation is a combination of objects, each of which is a setting forth of the real presence of the Logos in one of those aspects —infinite in number—which go to make up His glorious beauty ; and that the scene as a whole pos-sesses a unity and completeness of its own, arising from the fact of the prevailing Presence ; the contempla-tion of Nature has for him an effect of elevation of

---

[1] Liddon's *Bampton Lectures*, 1866, 5th Ed., p. 265.
[2] Notes on Col. i. 17.

soul, and a possibility of delight, far exceeding anything which it can inspire when regarded from any other point of view. The same would be the case with separate objects, the tiny flower, the lofty tree, the flake of snow, the massive precipice. The contemplation of the various aspects of Divine beauty thus pictured in corresponding presentments of natural beauty would no doubt prove the most fascinating and inspiring exercise of which the mind was capable.

It may seem strange to say so, but it is none the less certain that anything like a real apprehension of the beauties of natural scenery is a very rare thing ; that is to say, anything more than a mere vague sense of unintelligent admiration, or admiration which is devoid of intelligent appreciation of those features in which the beauties of the scene or object in question really consist. The study of Ruskin's works would be an unfailing means of convincing any reader of this fact. The taste for natural scenery is one which, like most of the more elevating forms of taste, needs cultivation for its development. And in the view before us, its cultivation would tend as well to the realisation of the love of God as to the increase of the joy of life, in a degree greater possibly than can be attained by any other branch of study.

The idea of the immanence of God is the leading principle underlying Hebrew poetry, and in that sense peculiar to itself. The idea is not so much that of an invisible power energising the various operations of nature, as that of a vast Personality, human in its character, and carrying on its operations (the phenomena of the natural world) by means of human actions, effected by human limbs and human organs. The idea pervades the whole Psalter, but nowhere finds expression more vividly and with greater variety of imagery than in the 104th Psalm, in which a general view is given of all the various operations of the physical universe instanced as effected by direct human-like action on the part of God, and their result as the setting forth of His glory and the manifestation of His own joy. In response to this we have the attitude of the creature as contemplating with uplifted, enraptured soul these manifestations of the Divine glory and Divine love, and thus making himself a sharer in the Divine emotion. " My joy is (*not* shall be) in Jehovah." The mastering of this particular psalm is in itself a distinct and definite step to the sensible realisation, in a devotional sense, of God's presence, all-mighty and all-loving, in the varied phenomena of the natural world, and of the creature's joyous and loving response to the address that is made to it by that Presence.

It begins with an apostrophe to the Divine Nature —" Praise Jehovah, O my soul." We address the Divine Being in the view which, in the exhibition of His works, He impresses upon us of His glory and beauty. Then we go on to the picturing of a series of Divine actions manifested in the operations of the world of nature. The subject of this psalm is not that of the personal Word of God in His relation to the personal man, nor to the Church as His kingdom ; it is simply an enraptured utterance of the spirit of natural religion. We see Jehovah, as it were, an infinite man engaged in carrying out His operations in the natural universe.[1]   We begin with light, the curtain interposed

---

[1] A common view taken by critics is to the effect that Jehovah was regarded by the Israelites merely as their own national god, His dominion limited to His own peculiar nation, occupying a similar position to that ascribed to Moloch and Baal over the nations which

between the observer and the Personal Source of all light. (The writer was not thinking of the world as a globe, nor as an object holding a minor place in the scheme of creation ; the world was to him the " be-all and end-all " of the universe, a level surface of immeasurable extent with the heavens as a dome-like canopy reaching over it.) Next is pictured to us the peopling of the world by the animal creation, and also the world of vegetation provided for its sustenance and comfort. " The earth is filled (perhaps satiated) with the fruit of Thy works." Those creatures are included whose dwelling is in uncultivated wastes, the mountains and craggy rocks, which are beyond man's reach and dominion. The climax is reached in the appearance of man himself, and the outburst of praise for which this forms the signal—" O Jehovah, how manifold are Thy works ; in wisdom hast Thou made them all, the earth is full of Thy riches."

The early Hebrews had no other Bible than the Book of Nature. It was their converse with nature which inspired within them the realisation of what Jehovah was in His essential Personality, as well as

owned allegiance to them. This view is probably true as regards the earlier periods of Hebrew History : Jehovah was, indeed, all in all to His own people, only because He was their God and Champion as against the gods of other nations. This, however, is far from being the view taken by the Hebrew poets. In this psalm, for instance, Jehovah is contemplated as nothing less than the God Who created and controls the whole universe. He deals first with light as a source of all being, then proceeds to the firmament and to the reservoirs in the upper waters from which the rain comes. The Omnipresence of Jehovah is recognised throughout. (We are reminded of the wonderful presentment of this fact exhibited in the chariot of the cherubim described by Ezekiel, the four-faced *zoa* with their attendant wheels as the means of bearing the Divine Presence with lightning speed in all directions over the whole universe. Ezek. i. 4–25.) At every turn the Divine Being is spoken of as performing the operations of physical nature with a human-like action. Jehovah is treated as the Great Artificer.

in His relations to themselves. They were brought near to God through their nearness to nature. It is possible that the most effective result of the study of the Psalms, as regards its practical application to the exercise of the devotional life, may be found in this spontaneous yet deliberate recognition of the real presence of the Divine Logos in the external world of nature. The practice of this spiritual converse with nature as a direct factor in the exercise of the devotional habit has hitherto, no doubt, received but little attention. Possibly indeed it belongs to such an advanced period of intellectual thought as that upon which the world appears to be entering at the present day ; and yet it is no new principle of devotional thought. The Hebrew poets, as we have seen, realised the Personal Presence of Jehovah everywhere throughout creation ; and not only as a Presence, but as an active, operating influence, and as inspired by a spirit of conscious benevolent interest in the phenomena of nature, and causing these phenomena by the direct action of His own will.

As a reason for the introduction of this subject in connection with that which is now before us—the formation and maintenance of the devotional habit— I would remind my readers of the fact of the remarkable approach which is being made nowadays between the material world on the one side, and the intellectual and spiritual world on the other, as one of the results which are being brought about by developments in the study of popular science. We may, perhaps, predicate that this tendency of study is promising to bring about the restoration of the great world of external nature, and the Bible which it represents, to its due place in the spiritual life, in spiritual education,

and in worship. The principle which underlies this
tendency is that to which I have referred as the thought
of the Real Presence of the Divine Logos in every
object of beauty, symmetry, and order that presents
itself to our senses in the external world. The thought
to be realised is that of the Divine Presence, as it were,
looking forth out of every such object ; speaking forth
out of it ; nay, more, giving itself in one of the corresponding aspects of its own beauty to the ready
observer.

This view of the Divine Presence is, of course,
realised by the Christian student in a much deeper and
fuller sense than was the case with the Hebrew poet.
It is the fact of the Incarnation which brings about
this closer touch, this fuller apprehension, leading the
observer to recognise the Divine Presence not only
as presiding, ruling, operating, but as *actually taking
into union with itself the universe of nature*, and so
bringing about a living touch with the seeker, and one
of closer character than could otherwise be effected.
Through our Lord's union with humanity He has taken
the whole world of nature into contact with Himself.
It is for us to look for, and admire, each object through
which He looks, speaks, gives Himself, and to realise
what in His Person—what special aspect of His
beauty—it pictures for us. It is for us to adore Him
Whose presence and Whose love towards us it depicts,
and so to make each such object a means of living
and loving personal contact with Him.

This spiritual study of the presence of Christ
pervading the world of nature in such a manner as to
convey itself in living communion to all who devoutly
seek Him there naturally leads up to that aspect of
this Real Presence which forms the supreme act of

contact between itself and the true receiver, namely, the Sacrament of His Body and Blood, wherein the all-pervading Presence finds, as it were, its focus. The Presence is as real, as literal, when considered as disseminated in the various departments of its operation throughout the universe as it is in the Sacrament, but in the latter we find that Presence, so to speak, in its fulness ; that is to say, presenting Itself in such a form as to communicate not some one or other of His innumerable qualities of grace and love as in other features of His immanence, but His whole Self in the entire complex of all those constituent qualities and graces which belong to the Divine Humanity. Here we have the climax of the grand idea of the Real Presence of the Logos in His creation.

PART II

THE PRIEST'S CARE OF THE SOULS UNDER HIS CHARGE

" Προσέχετε ἑαυτοῖς καὶ παντὶ τῷ ποιμνίῳ, . . .
ποιμαίνειν τὴν ἐκκλησίαν τοῦ Θεοῦ, ἣν περιεποιήσατο
διὰ τοῦ αἵματος τοῦ ἰδίου."

Acts xx. 28.

THE PRIEST'S RELATIONS WITH HIS PEOPLE

ONE object to be aimed at by the priest is that of placing himself on terms of personal relationship and confidence with every individual in his parish. This may seem an ideal to be aimed at rather than a result to be attained with any probability, except in small congregations ; yet it must be aimed at and striven for might and main. For example, the priest should never lose an opportunity of speaking pastorally to any member of his flock who may chance to come his way. In his visits to homes he must often miss the men, since they are so frequently absent from various causes : yet they must be the chief object of his attention. Never, therefore, let him lose the opportunity of an interview, and let him see that every opportunity is properly utilised to the effect that something is said which is likely to be of real benefit. Care must be taken also not to repel by anything like abruptness or a dictatorial manner ; his part is to win souls, angle for them, entrap them :—

" ἀνθρώπους ἔσῃ ζωγρῶν."—St. Luke v. 10.
" ἁλιεῖς ἀνθρώπων."—St. Matt. iv. 19.

We are often told that the parson's society is rather avoided by the average male member of his flock, and especially by the young men. He must make it the

63

first care to do away with the possibility of such a feeling in those who belong to him ; his efforts for their good will certainly be neutralised if this state of affairs is permitted to exist. And let the priest assure himself that if such a sentiment of repulsion does exist the fault lies with himself. In very few cases will even the shyest and most apparently impracticable member be able to resist the advances made in the kindly, open-hearted, affectionate manner which is the outcome of a true, heartfelt, loving interest in the individual. He should, of course, avoid anything like preaching or laying down the law in his manner towards the members of his flock. Let him acquire the habit of entering so fully into the personal interests and concerns of his people that he may always find something to say to each individual which will enlist his interest and good will. At the same time, while such overtures will generally, in the first place at least, deal with temporal concerns, he must never lose sight of the fact that his attitude is to be always that of watching for souls. In every conversation this object should be kept in view, and the opportunity sought or made for the introduction of some element of spiritual guidance and admonition. This is especially needful in the case of those whom he is likely to meet but seldom, whilst in these instances particularly special care is necessary to avoid anything likely to have a disconcerting or repellent effect upon them. Make it a rule, if possible, never to send a man away with a feeling of displeasure towards you, but let him leave you in such a frame of mind that he will be glad to see you again. Even in cases in which rebuke has to be administered it does not necessarily follow that such a friendly parting is impossible. Be loving and gentle in your reproofs and then you can generally be as severe as you like. Combine the authority of a priest with the sympathy of a fellow creature and the humility of a fellow sinner.

Be specially careful to know the children and to gain their confidence. Learn and bear in mind their names separately, so as to be able to address them personally ; this will be found a great means of winning not only their regard and trust, but also that of their parents. Teach them to come to you and talk to you ; let them have a considerable share of your direct attention. Be sure to make inquiry with reference to their practice of saying their prayers, attendance at Sunday School, or other important duties.

ON THE PRACTICE OF AURICULAR CONFESSION

IT is an unquestioned fact that a strong and very general prejudice exists against what is known by the term " Auricular Confession." Nor is this prejudice altogether ill-founded. We cannot afford to decry or even ignore it. The thing which it contemplates and which represents its idea of the practice in question is certainly objectionable. In any case there are very serious dangers attending the practice we shall now consider, namely, that which we may describe as Sacramental Confession.

As ordinarily practised it is altogether too slight a thing, conducted too hurriedly, and therefore superficial. This is rendered inevitable from the fact of the numbers who have to be dealt with, and possibly in some cases by the frequency with which it is observed. In most cases, however, it is the rarity rather than the frequency of observance which tends to neutralise any benefit which might otherwise attend its use. The idea of compressing the acknowledgment of a year's sin and the presentment of the comprehensive view of the soul's condition as arrived at in that period, together with the admonition and direction which would necessarily arise as its result, all within the space of say half an hour, or even an hour, involves a self-evident absurdity. The truly discreet and learned priest will generally find more than one interview necessary for the purpose. The various avenues through which the central principle of sin finds its vent, and the various concrete forms which it takes in so doing, will have to be traced and dealt with separately ; then the various aspects which the central principle of " love-motive " will have to assume in the work of correcting the mischief in its different shapes must also be set before the penitent fully and distinctly. This will require time for thought and for the initiation of act. Hence the practice of sacramental confession for any individual, in such a degree as to promise real benefit, must necessarily be occasional and comparatively infrequent.

Another danger connected with this practice is that of leading the penitent to place too much dependence upon a human mediator, more especially in the act of Absolution. It is therefore most essential that the priest should clearly explain his position as that of a mere agent, whose office is simply that of leading the penitent to recognise and address himself to the Real Presence of the one great Confessor, Absolver, and Director, Who is invisible. A fearful responsibility rests upon the officiating agent in this respect. He must bear in mind the tendency in weak humanity to turn aside from the invisible to the visible, to depend upon earthly props and supports ; he must remember the danger of hindering rather than helping the work of salvation by assisting to deflect the penitent's view from the One Object, the contemplation of which brings life. He must make absolutely sure that throughout the whole course of this sacramental proceeding the penitent has his eye fixed upon the invisible High Priest, and that in every act which he is called upon to perform—whether it be confession, renunciation, or loving trust—it is Christ Himself Whom he is addressing, while the earthly priest stands aside as it were, and simply leads and points the penitent to the true Personal Object of every spiritual endeavour.

Again, there is the danger of arousing the spirit of prejudice to which reference has been made, and so repelling the penitent, and incurring the loss of influence in a general sense. The priest should bear in mind the fact that prejudice, though unreasonable, may not be despised or disregarded ; it is one of the most serious hindrances to the priest's influence for good ; it should therefore be his care, and the object of strenuous effort, to allay or disarm it. He cannot fight it down, that is certain. He must be patient with it, treat it as a disease, and above all things treat it with gentleness and kindness. If he cannot allay or remove it let him assure himself that the fault must be to a great extent his own. Remember St. Aidan—"Was it their stubbornness or your severity ? Did you forget the Apostle's command to feed them first with milk and then with meat ? " [1] There are, however, few instances in which the parish priest need get to loggerheads with his people if he can only bring himself to act as St. Aidan acted. So with confession ; the most desirable method of conducting it is, no doubt, in the Church, the priest habited in cassock, surplice, and stole. But supposing that the practice in this form should be objectionable to a portion of his flock, simply because they associate it (and not unreasonably) with methods of conducting it which he himself would probably

[1] Wakeman, *History of the Church of England*, 7th edit. p. 24.

allow to be open to serious objection, he would show himself to be an unwise pastor by persisting in conducting it with those particular adjuncts.   He would find no difficulty in gaining his point as regards the true nature of the sacrament if he could only bring himself to dispense with what cannot be regarded as in any sense essential features.

It is true that many of his people, especially those who need it the most, would object to yielding their confidence to their clergyman on the subject of their inner life.   This is a difficulty of an entirely different character, and is to be overcome only by the exercise of personal influence of such a kind as to invite and win their confidence through the manifestation on the priest's part of a character worthy of being admitted to such inner relations.

But when all is said and done, the great obstacle to the profitable exercise of this all-important priestly function consists in too many instances in the lack of qualification on the priest's part for that exercise. Rome has its cut-and-dried method in which its clergy are fully instructed.   They know exactly what they have to do, and they do it accordingly.   To us their performance of this sacramental ordinance may appear lamentably inadequate, but that is their business, not ours.   With our fuller light—as we are taught to regard it—we could not dare to enter upon the practice of sacramental confession on the same lines as those which they follow.   We realise the necessity for going deeper and riding higher, and this being so, we forego it altogether and leave our young members to flounder along as best they may !   Brethren, this ought not so to be.   Then why is it so?   Simply because the due observance of the practice entails qualifications which are not possessed in sufficient kind and degree by the average parish priest. Such qualifications are :—

(1) A knowledge of human nature attainable only by careful study and by experience founded upon watchful observations, digested by mature judgment.

(2) The main requisite of personal knowledge of our Lord Himself, in His character as Example, and in His relation to humanity as a Lover of souls.

Training in the former respects should form a conspicuous feature in the preparation of candidates for Holy Orders, and although the shortness of the time ordinarily allowed for such preparation would make it impossible to carry out this form of study with any degree of thoroughness, yet the instruction given in this subject should have the effect of giving the student a start in the pursuit of this all-important branch of study. The young clergyman in his Diaconate and early Priesthood should make it one of the most emphatic objects of his study and efforts to carry on the work of training himself in this branch of his duty, and this not necessarily by the use of books on this special subject, which are often misleading. Better means are those of self-examination, careful observation, meditation, and the practice of the Presence of our Lord. Careful observation, not of course in the sense of prying or espionage, but open and above-board, such as will infallibly be attained by the habit of spiritual conversation with all sorts of people, and with each one in that particular manner and tone which individually suits him best. The young priest cannot be too cautious in the matter of entering upon the discharge of this branch of his functions. The very greatest mischief may be the result of his taking it up with " 'prentice hand." The human soul is a frail and delicate piece of texture to handle, and the work of operating upon it calls for the surgeon's hand—a symbol which represents the ideal of the priestly art—firm, unshrinking, unshaking, strong, decided—yet gentle as a woman's.

THE TREATMENT OF INDIVIDUAL SOULS

ONE of the great needs in the training of candidates for Holy Orders is some systematised and specialised instruction in the method of treatment for individual souls. The practice of Confession is referred to in the Exhortation in the Communion Service, as well as in the rubric in the Office for the Visitation of the Sick. The priest's duty in this respect is a form of pastoral work to his preparation for which too little regard has been paid in the past. It is to be feared that the systematic observance of the conduct of private confessions has to a large extent fallen into disuse, or, still worse, has been undertaken by those whose capacity for such delicate work is more than doubtful. Before venturing upon this duty a large degree of acquaintance with human nature in its inner depths and in its varied forms of development is required on the part of the practitioner. Incalculable mischief has resulted from the taking in hand of this form of pastoral work by those who were inadequately fitted for it. How is this fitness to be attained ?

In the first place the practitioner must study the subject in relation to his own soul, remembering that in its main features human nature is always the same.

The duty of self-examination must be explained and strictly enforced. Not only must your instruction to this effect be given clearly and wisely, but you must watch its results. Beware of false diffidence in inviting and urging confidence; remember the absolute necessity for free and unrestrained intercourse between penitent and priest on the subject of the spiritual condition and of spiritual difficulties. Be on the watch for indications of a desire to open the heart to you, and be on the alert to meet it more than half-way; otherwise you may lose golden opportunities. Better risk repulse than miss the chance of saving, or even helping, a soul.

You will often find that the desire for the relief arising from such confidential dealing has long been existent in the heart, and only restrained by timidity or diffidence. In such cases the penitent is often, owing to the priest's neglect, driven to seek relief in other quarters, from more faithful if less qualified confidants. The attainment of the person's confidence must be regarded as indispensable, must be aimed at, planned for, striven for, prayed for. Until it has been attained the priest can hardly consider his ministrations, so far as regards the case in question, as other than a failure.

The practice of confession may be regarded as having two forms. The first is that which may be called Plenary Confession, or the confession which is made by one who, for the first time in any real and complete sense, seeks reconciliation with God, and entrance upon the definite practice of the spiritual life. He may be a baptised person who has not lived up to his baptismal vocation; at all events, he is one who has never yet fairly and definitely sought and attained the condition of reconciliation with God. The second form of confession is that which is made by one to whom the act of conscious approach to God and of yielding up the soul to Him for pardon and grace is not a new one, but who has already known what it is to experience the gift of absolution at former periods in his life, with greater or less frequency and regularity.

In the first of these two cases the penitent is, of course, required to look back upon his entire life past. He is carrying about with him, unabsolved, the whole burden of a life's sin, and must realise that burden in its entirety before bringing it to the foot of the cross for the double gift of absolution and cleansing. To call to mind all the sins of a lifetime, or even any considerable fraction of them, is manifestly impossible. But it is none the less necessary, by dint of careful research and self-examination, to arrive at an idea of the general tenor of that special form of sin which has characterised the individual's life ; and also to call to mind the leading special acts of sin to which the conscience testifies as standing out prominently in his life's history. This process of research will call for the exercise of great care and unremitting attention, so as to make the confession sufficiently comprehensive to represent a true view of the life's sin. Of course, the object sought in leading a sinner to open out the secrets of his heart to Christ, whether it be directly or through the agency of the human priest, is not that of (as it were) informing the Lord Himself, or even the earthly priest, on the subject. It is rather that of bringing before the penitent's own view a sufficiently full and comprehensive idea of his condition as a sinner before God, as to awaken within him the sentiment of heartfelt repentance, and a fervent desire for cleansing from the guilt of sin and release from its yoke. Hence definite and particular confession is necessary, whether the confession is made to Christ Himself alone or to the priest as His representative.

As a matter of fact, the disuse of so-called " auricular confession," which took place after the Reformation, has too often led to the disuse of real confession in any sense whatever. A man is satisfied with acknowledging in a general way his condition as a·sinner, without realising in any true sense what that condition means, namely, what those sins are for which he asks forgiveness. The omission is a most dangerous one, if not even fatal. In the first place, the sinner fails in the comprehension of the character and heinousness of the sins of which he supposes himself to repent ; and hence, it is questionable whether his repentance can possess that depth and reality which is needful to make it fully effectual. In the second place, the lack of self-examination into the various forms of sin which most easily beset him will tend to deprive him of that knowledge of those sins which is needful to enable him to guard against them for the future. Hence, fulness and explicitness in self-examination and expression of sin is to be carefully enforced from the outset.

The presentment of the sins of a lifetime as an act of penitence before the cross of Christ by one who has never definitely performed such an act in the past forms a crisis in his life, calling for the most solemn attention and care at the hands of both penitent and practitioner. The preparation for it must necessarily take a considerable time ; anything like haste or lack of due deliberation may be fatal. Some amount even of delay may be found necessary to enable the penitent to arrange fully and clearly before his own view the consciousness of his condition and needs as a sinner, and also to make sure of his mind as regards his desire for new life, and his purpose to set about it. Yet should delay be found necessary, it is imperative that there should be no slackening in his efforts after attaining the consummation he desires, for such slackening will generally mean falling away. The penitent should be warned that his sincerity may be tried by apparent delay in the inward response made to his efforts after reconciliation with God. It is by such delay that the winnowing process is effected, whereby those who are but half-hearted drop off and show themselves unworthy of the gift which they wish for and affect to seek. The failure is simply because the seeker is not really in earnest. Some response, however, in the way of a comforting sense of acceptance will always be in some degree vouchsafed.

The penitent should be taught to distinguish between faith and assurance. Faith does not mean, nor does it imply, the presence of assurance. Faith may be accompanied by much doubt. Faith means the acceptance at God's hands of a gift which God has promised to bestow on certain conditions. Faith is simply the fulfilment of those conditions. Faith is an act always, not a feeling. Belief is not faith, nor any part of faith, although it is essential to lead a man to perform the act of self-surrender in which faith really consists.

As has already been intimated, the priest must ascertain from the penitent the scope of the confession to be made, whether it should include the whole of his past life, or whether it simply looks back to some former act of confession which has been complete of its kind, and followed by a full and satisfactory absolution. It will, of course, come to the same thing, whether this has been done by the aid of a priest, or by direct communication with our Lord Himself. The latter, no doubt, is by far the best method when the penitent is sufficiently nurtured in the spiritual life to be qualified to practise it. Moreover, it should be the priest's declared aim to assist the penitent in attaining such a degree of maturity as will enable him to dispense with the services of an earthly practitioner in this particular respect. Yet it is most desirable, especially in the case of the young (that is, of boys), that the practice of direct auricular confession should be revived, though in such a form as not to rouse a prejudice in those who might otherwise be disposed to take alarm.

The priest should, however, beware of keeping the penitent in leading strings longer than is necessary. There can be no doubt that the more excellent way is that of direct, personal confession to a Personal Christ. The practice of retaining a penitent in the observance of auricular confession longer than is necessary may be attended by three evils.

(1) It may tend to cultivate an effeminate type of life, and hinder the development of the masculine qualities of judgment, discretion, and self-control.

(2) It may be an obstacle to that direct and confidential communion with the Personal Christ which is the ideal of the spiritual life.

(3) Even supposing it were the best way, yet when we consider the comparatively very small number of priests who are qualified to administer this sacrament, one has to take into account the danger accruing to the penitent in case of his removal to a place where

there is no priest duly qualified for this purpose, if his training has made him dependent upon this practice for the sustenance of his spiritual life.

No priest should be satisfied with taking up a case which has formerly been dealt with by another priest, and following it on the identical lines observed by his predecessor, unless his own judgment commends this course as suitable and sufficient in the particular case before him. Each priest has his own separate responsibility, his own judicial position, for the exercise of which he must answer directly to his Master. Supposing one who has been in the habit of regular confession should come to him for this purpose, the priest must satisfy himself by careful inquiry that the man's spiritual life is in a state suitable for the bestowal of absolution, before he consents to pronounce it. If his predecessor has been in the practice, only too common, of a superficial treatment of souls, the priest must beware of confirming his mistakes, perhaps to the fatal injury of an immortal soul. Let him beware of the condemnation of " healing the hurt of the daughter of my people slightly, saying, Peace, peace ; when there is no peace." [1] He must be deep and searching in his inquiries as to the consciousness of sin as a reality in its inner depths and springs, as well as in certain external exhibitions of a more or less serious character. At the same time, let him beware of making the smallest shade of reflection, directly or indirectly, on a brother priest, for any neglect or incompetence he may have shown in his dealing with the penitent.

The priest must be on his guard against manifesting anything like disgust or repulsion, whatever the nature of the sin may be. Deepest seriousness, and the fullest

[1] Jer. viii. 11.

sense of heinousness, may be combined with the tenderest gentleness and the utmost kindliness. Remember the very fact that the penitent comes to you with his offering of humble acknowledgment, that he is of his own accord, and so far as he can do so, opening his heart to your view, entitles him to your deepest personal interest and regard. Let it be seen that the acknowledgment of his sin does not repel you from him, but draws you closer to him. In any case, *you* cannot judge the relative degrees of criminality ; forms which to you may seem grossest, may possibly, in God's sight, be less offensive than others which may appear to you to be comparatively slight.

You have invited your penitent to such a degree of confidence as he may think well to repose in you, or you may think well to seek from him. How closely you may press such investigation will, of course, depend upon your own judgment, and this will call for the nicest discrimination. The question whether he should be urged to make a full and complete disclosure of his spiritual condition calls for careful consideration on your part. You have to satisfy yourself that, if he does not commit himself wholly into your hands, he is capable of taking care of himself ; that is to say, of entering by his own individual efforts into such direct and close intercourse with our Lord as his Confessor, Absolver, and Director, as will be sufficient for the maintenance of his spiritual life. This is ideally the best condition which a Christian can attain ; and to help him in attaining this is the chief object which the priest should have in view.

Supposing he fails to show any disposition to yield his full confidence, and yet you feel that he is not capable of taking care of himself, what are you to do ?

You cannot force his confidence. The cause of his reserve very probably lies in the fact that what is being concealed is some very serious form of spiritual disease, lying possibly at the very root of his character, and calling for full and drastic treatment as essential to his salvation. Hence you cannot afford to disregard any symptoms which would seem to point to such a condition of things, and, leaving these unattended to, pass on to deal with other matters. It will generally be the case that those features of soul-sickness which a man is most indisposed to reveal, are just those very features which most strongly call for disclosure for the purpose of spiritual treatment. Yet you cannot force a man's confidence.

Bear in mind the two main objects of your efforts :—

First, the endeavour by kindly and gentle but searching inquiry to ascertain the real condition of the man's soul towards God, with a view to leading him to ascertain it for himself, and so to recognise in himself the nature of that element of sin which is the barrier between himself and God.

Secondly, the endeavour to point out to him as the Object of his loving trust, and of his grasp by faith, the Personal Christ, as the Forgiver of his sin and the Cleanser from its stain.

The process may be difficult and tedious, but if it is set about with serious earnestness, and persevered in with the determination not to give up, together with heartfelt prayer for guidance, success will generally be attained. At all events, the priest will have saved his own soul. The great difficulty is that of impressing upon the sinner an adequate consciousness of sin. How sadly familiar to the faithful priest, in response to his efforts gently to arouse that consciousness, is the vague and pointless rejoinder, " Yes, we are all sinners "! This expression in itself may almost be taken as a sign of failure hitherto in the effort to awaken anything like the sentiment of repentance. It is not until a man has been brought to say with the repentant king : " *I* have sinned against the Lord," [1] or with the publican : " God be merciful to *me* a sinner," [2] that he can be safely regarded as truly realising the nature of sin as affecting his own person. This is one of the main reasons calling for explicitness and categorical method in the confession of sin. A man hardly realises that he is a sinner, until his conscience points out to him what those sins are wherein his sinfulness consists, at least in their main features. In fact, we may almost say that it is only by contemplating instances of sin that the character of sin as a disease can be distinctly recognised.

It is true that there are forms of sin even the very glance at which may seem to carry with it a touch of defilement, and which must therefore be regarded as in a sense exceptions to the above rule. Nevertheless, these forms have to be dealt with, and it is in dealing with these that the highest degree of skill as exercised by a spiritual physician is called for. In dealing with women, unless called for by extreme urgency, this department should be altogether avoided. With men, however, the case is different. It is oftentimes in this particular department of temptation that the sinner stands in greatest need of help, and in which his confidence is to be most anxiously invited. Yet even in the case of male penitents absolute particulars should be avoided, although investigation should be

---

[1] 2 Sam. xii. 13a.   [2] St. Luke xviii. 13.

made into the degree and extent of the sin, its frequency of commission, and aggravating circumstances. The patient should, of course, be warned not to implicate any other person in his admissions ; he should also be discouraged from those efforts at mitigation and palliation, or excuse, which in so many cases hopelessly neutralise any advance toward true contrition.

Reference has been made to the necessity for contemplating sin in the form of definite and concrete acts in order to convey a distinct idea of its reality as sin, and its application to the individual, considered apart from the general infection of the human race at large. At the same time the priest must carefully avoid the very common mistake of allowing a confession to consist of a mere list of acts of commission or instances of omission. One great purpose of his investigation is that of penetrating below the external surface of the life of action and omission, into those inner depths of the soul where lie the springs of purpose and motive, and from which those active results really proceed. His aim must be, in the first place, to ascertain what is usually known as the besetting sin, which really means that peculiar bent of character which is proper to the individual, and which is the source of the good in him as well as the evil ; but which, human nature being what it is, more naturally tends to evil than to good. Something will be said a little later in reference to the different aspects of tendency such as are here signified.

The disclosure by the penitent of the different forms of sinful act or sinful omission of which he feels himself to be guilty, will be utilised by the priest to assist him in arriving at a diagnosis of the system of inward tendency or character which finds expression in those acts or omissions. Hence he deals with them, not as isolated entities, but as different symptoms of one underlying disease ; and his efforts are directed towards the disease itself, thus striking at the root of the varied results which it occasions. He must bear in mind, too, that it is not so much for his own information that these researches are being made, as for that of the penitent himself. The priest's object is to open the penitent's eyes to those sources from which proceed the various forms of evil which are tending to his ruin. Hence the mistake of simply assigning penance as a remedy, which may be more or less effectual, for a symptom, while yet the disease itself, from which as a plant or weed the symptom grows, is left untouched and unregarded. The symptoms have, of course, to be dealt with separately. Each outcome or aspect of evil needs careful consideration ; but that consideration should be based upon the inner cause from which all forms of sin, as manifested in that particular individual, spring. It must be borne in mind that the only true secret of successful conflict with sin consists in the substitution of the active principle of personal love for a Personal Christ in the place of the old principle of self-seeking or self-will. It is only by the expulsive effect of a new and nobler attachment that any real probability of victory over old and inveterate habit can be attained. This new love-principle then must be cultivated, and when fairly set on foot will be found the mightiest of all engines in spiritual conflict.

The priest should distinctly set before the penitent the fact that our Lord Himself, in His Personal Presence, is the true High Priest, and that the earthly priest's part is only that of assisting the penitent in bringing himself into direct communication with our Lord. It should be explained that since such official human intervention is often helpful, and sometimes necessary, you gladly offer yourself in your priestly capacity as the outward means for obtaining the inward and spiritual grace.

Instruct him next to open out his heart to you freely and completely, as a patient his case to his physician, assuring him that you can be of little use otherwise ; at the same time make it quite clear to him that he may depend absolutely upon your heartfelt sympathy, tender compassion, and inviolable confidence. The whole thing should be made as solemn as possible, and endued with the character of a religious act.

The attitude of the priest is that of sitting, except during prayer, absolution, and benediction. The attitude of the penitent is that of kneeling ; this, however, may, if it appear absolutely necessary on account of infirmity, be deviated from. The attitude of kneeling is requisite, because confession is being made to Christ Himself as personally present, and in a spirit of deepest humiliation. In all such cases regard must be paid to freedom from physical strain or uneasiness as the result of the posture maintained ; at all events, to such an extent as would be likely to hinder the free action of mind and spirit.

The priest will, of course, provide himself with a suitable Office for the purpose. He may possibly fail to find any at present published which will in all respects satisfy him. In this case he will have to compile one for himself, including possible extemporaneous prayer such as may give expression to the special requirements of the individual and the occasion. But if this is done, let the whole Office be carefully planned and pre-arranged. He will generally find it desirable to begin by prayer for himself, aloud, to the effect that the Great High Priest may guide him in dealing faithfully, wisely, tenderly, with this member of his flock, making him the means of aiding the penitent in drawing near to the Good Shepherd and opening his heart to His gracious view ; further, for the penitent, that he may be moved to open his heart fully, freely, and without reserve to him who now acts as Christ's unworthy representative ; that he may be led to confess fully sins committed, duties omitted, actions, words, and thoughts which have offended his purity ; that he may grieve for them, may turn from them, may cast them from him, may seek and obtain, at the Saviour's hands, the gift of pardon through His Blood, which may atone for the past. Then he will pray for the gift of His Spirit to convey grace and power to enable him to shun sin for the future, and to take up his cross of duty and self-denial and to follow in his Saviour's steps.

It will be observed that the object at present in view is that of avoiding formality, and the observance of stereotyped forms and methods, whilst maintaining unimpaired the full essence of the sacrament. It is not, therefore, thought desirable to insist upon the use by the penitent in the act of confession of the ordinary cut-and-dried formula ; though if such has been his previous custom, there is no reason why he should not follow it. In any case, the priest himself may prefer that he should be instructed to do so. This, of course, is a matter of indifference. The formula should not be used if it is likely to arouse unfavourable prejudice

on the part of the penitent or others. The priest
who truly cares for his flock will ever be tender in
dealing with them, and on his guard against inflicting
a wound, however slight, and however unreasonable
be the state of feeling which renders the person sus-
ceptible to it. We will therefore suppose him entering upon the subject of confession in a kindly but
serious manner, somewhat as follows :—

" Now let us address ourselves to the subject before
us. You have come to open out your heart to me,
who am a sinner like yourself, but to whom God has
entrusted the charge of watching for and caring for
the souls which belong to Him. Let me ask you to
open out your heart to me. Do it as in the presence
of our Saviour Himself, Who is truly present, and
Who is the True Confessor. What I say to you I shall
try to say as though He said it, because I am here as
His representative, His spokesman. Utterly unworthy
though I am, and needing, as I do, just what you
need, try to think of yourself as speaking to Him and
listening to Him."

The penitent will need careful assistance in making
his confession. The priest may begin by asking him
his own view of his condition as regards the relation
of his soul to God. (We are now supposing a person
who is making his first confession to this particular
priest.) Of course, his first inquiry is with reference
to any former confession which the penitent may have
made ; and, such having been the case, the priest
will have to make further inquiry for his own guidance
as to whether he is safe in taking that former confession as the starting-point of his own investigation.
The first thing would be to ascertain the present
position of the penitent's soul towards God, *i.e.*

whether he may be regarded as living in any real sense the spiritual life—a life in which the governing presence of God is realised, and which is being consciously submitted to that governance. If this is the case, it will generally be possible to trace the last full performance of a definite act of self-examination, confession, and absolution to some definite period, which may be taken as the starting-point of the new period of investigation.

The priest must beware of satisfying himself with inquiry into specific instances of sin, and overlooking the duty which should stand foremost in the work he is engaged in, namely, that of ascertaining whether the love of God, together with humble trust in Christ Jesus, is actively present in the heart of the penitent. In other words, *is his life a converted one ?* [1]

(*a*) Is the life which the penitent is now leading the result of conversion on his part, considered as an act of his own—or possibly as a course of action ? It is of imperative importance that the priest should at the outset make sure of the state of things in this respect.

(*b*) Is the life of the penitent one which is being led " in the Spirit," in however imperfect a manner, and not " in the flesh," that is, in a state of bondage

---

[1] This word " conversion " is, perhaps, of all the words in the practice of religion, the one most entirely misunderstood ; the result, no doubt, of a gross mistranslation of the word where it occurs in Scripture. How it has been allowed to pass from generation to generation uncorrected is inexplicable. It is needful to be clear on this point. There is, strictly speaking, no such thing as *being* converted. In Acts iii. 19, the word which St. Peter used in the passage rendered in our Authorised Version, " *Repent*, therefore, and be converted," is given in the Greek as ἐπιστρέψατε, a word which can mean nothing less than " turn about." Conversion is an action, not an experience ; something to be done, not to be asked for ; though the grace and power to do it may, of course, be subjects for prayer.

to the lower nature ? Plain direct questioning will be necessary to elicit the truth on this subject, but it will be useless to proceed until this point has been cleared up.

(c) Is the penitent a child of God who has already yielded up his allegiance to God as his Ruler and Guide, or is he only an inquirer seeking after that condition as not yet having attained it ? It is very possible that the penitent may hitherto have deceived himself on this subject, as well as possibly his spiritual directors. His efforts at religion thus far may have been of the most superficial character, not having included the actual giving up of his heart to the love and service of God.

The question in brief may be expressed as follows : Can you say that you are now conducting your life with a direct view to fulfilling the will of God in so doing, and of subduing your own will when it is in opposition to His ? Is this the set purpose of your present life, even though you know it to be hindered by many shortcomings and failures ?

Suppose that the penitent should be able to answer in the affirmative, and to satisfy the priest that he is justified in doing so, the course of the confession will proceed accordingly. But let the priest remember the very serious danger, and let me say even probability, of self-deception on the part of the penitent in this respect. The responsibility of his director in this point is very serious. The danger of confirming the inquirer in his self-deception, and thus hindering instead of helping the hope of his salvation, is one that may well dismay a spiritual director. He trembles as he remembers the Lord's awful saying : " If the blind lead the blind, *both* shall fall into the ditch."

¹ St. Matt. xv. 14.

Should the answers have turned out to be really satisfactory, the priest's further task is comparatively easy ; he will, none the less, need careful and close examination to assist the penitent in realising, it may be, even the nature of his besetting sin. The degree of ignorance oftentimes exhibited on this subject, even in those who are really heart and soul Christians, is well-nigh incredible. This point will, therefore, have to be carefully taken up, and the penitent assisted to trace the various developments of the central sin in the different forms of sinful act and sinful omission which characterise his life. He must be taught in all respects to judge himself, to watch himself, to maintain a continual attitude of alertness. He must be taught that the universal antidote for every form of deflection from the course of duty is to be found in the love of Christ, that is, love for Christ. He must learn to apply this antidote in its different aspects to each department of need, coming to understand how various forms and developments of love are capable, by varied application, of overpowering corresponding forms of evil ; how self-love [1] is only to be expelled by bringing against it the application of higher love.

Let us suppose however that, as will most generally be the case, the priest is led to the conclusion that the inquirer has not yet *converted* his life, but is still living under the control of his lower nature, even though he may sincerely desire to be set free from the tyrant's yoke. His first duty is, of course, to set clearly before the penitent the object which is to be attained,

---

[1] The term " self-love," however, it is to be observed, is a misnomer, strictly speaking. Love means outgoing from self. There are such things as self-gratification, and so forth, but there is really no such thing as self-love. (See 2 Cor. v. 14, and 2 Cor. x. 5 in the Greek.)

namely, the love of Christ, and participation in that life of glory and purity and beauty which is Christ's as the result of His Incarnation ; by which latter term is meant the act of His taking into communion with Himself in His infinite Godhead the nature of man in its entirety, in order that by that definite contact it might be transformed and infused with His own life and restored to mankind in its ennobled and glorified condition.   Of course this grand and mysterious truth is set before the inquirer in such a form, and with such a degree of child-like plainness and simplicity, as may be necessary in order to enable him to take it in such a manner as to assist him to realise its application to himself as answering to the deepest cravings of his nature.   He will generally be slow in grasping this aspect of saving truth.   The motive most usual in bringing a sinner to his knees is that of mere selfish fear ; its question is, " What must I do to be saved ? " —a distinctly selfish motive.   Nor, as we may believe, is even this selfish approach necessarily rejected.   Even though the sinner be rather driven to Christ by his fears than drawn to Him by his affections, he will not on that account be excluded.   If the higher motives will not suffice to bring him to Christ, a lower one may have this effect ; if he cannot go to Him as the Magi did, " with the offering of a free heart," at all events he may approach Him as " fleeing from the wrath to come." [1]   Yet, though self-interest be the first motive for the approach, it cannot be really effective in attaining its object unless the penitent proceed to the further step of seeking Love by an effort which has an element of love within it.   There is profound signi-ficance in those words of our Lord, " Her sins, which

[1] St. Matt. iii. 7.

are many, are forgiven ; *for she loved much.*" [1] The priest's endeavour, therefore, would be to set before the penitent, as far as he is capable of receiving it, this particular aspect of the work of salvation—the invitatory attitude of a loving Saviour, rather than the mere offer of deliverance from a dreaded penalty. This is the ideal method of approach, though, in the majority of cases perhaps, he will find the inquirer incapable of apprehending it at the outset.

One great requisite in dealing with a penitent at this early stage is that of tenderness and consideration, not expecting too much, nor too rapid an advance. The priest finds him, at all events, " grieved and wearied with the burden of his sin " ; or it may be perhaps hardly even " grieved " ; rather oppressed and terrified, seeking safety, that is, release from penalty rather than release from the power, and cleansing from the stain of the sin itself. It is to this latter point, therefore, that his attention is first directed, and he will find his chief difficulty in the effort to impress upon the inquirer a sense of the heinousness of sin as considered in itself, and quite apart from penal consequences that may be threatened. One who has not taken this form of pastoral work in hand can form no idea of the difficulty which is often experienced in bringing about the result which is now under consideration. The fact of realising it as a difficulty to be dealt with, yes, struggled with, is perhaps the best means of guiding the priest in fitting himself to encounter it. He feels that the whole welfare of his undertaking depends upon his success in leading the inquirer to make from his heart spontaneously the free confession : " I have sinned against the Lord "—consciousness of doing despite to a

[1] St. Luke vii. 47.

Father's love—that is the only view of sin which can lead to repentance in any true sense. To this point therefore, the director is seeking to guide his pupil ; how it is to be done must depend in great measure upon his own judgment ; his success in so doing will depend very greatly upon his own personal interest in the matter, his sympathy with the penitent, and his own attainment as regards love for the Lord. Intense earnestness will be necessary on his own part as a means of conveying the same sentiment to his hearer. There is nothing so contagious as real earnestness unless it be real indifference. The priest should bear this fact in mind throughout, in order that it may consciously influence his treatment of his patient.

Nowadays we may recognise a special unwillingness to realise and recognise sin as a serious barrier between the soul and God ; it is rather looked upon as a misfortune, as an obstacle to a man's own welfare. Hence the necessity of enforcing the conception of the love of God as requiring the response of love on the part of the creature which is its object. Sin consists in wilfully " grieving the Holy Spirit of God whereby ye are sealed " [1]—sealed with the seal of a Father's love. The inquirer should be led to recognise his sin in its twofold effect—

(1) That of defilement, making him an object unfit for the Father's loving view.

(2) That of crippling, paralysing his capability for effort after good, after carrying out that work of love which belongs to his position as a child of a loving Father.

He must be shown that God is " of purer eyes than to behold evil," [2] and that evil in any form must

[1] Eph. iv. 30.   [2] Hab. i. 13.

necessarily be offensive to the eyes of Him with Whom the law of Order—which is Love—is the law of His own Person, and the law of the universe of His realm. Sin is nothing more and nothing less than a breach, wilful and deliberate, of this universal law which is not only God's, but which also is God Himself, namely, that *perfect order which is love*. Sin consists in being out of harmony with the All-harmonious.

It is not proposed that the priest should endeavour to instil these particular sentiments into the mind of his patient, but rather that his own soul be possessed with them and directed by the spirit which would be the necessary outcome of a loving consciousness of these grand truths.

Now would come the enumeration of acts and habits of personal sin in the way of commission and omission, and including sins of thought, word and deed. These should be dealt with, as has already been urged, in relation to the main principle lying at the root of all —the love or non-love of God. Hence, as has been already intimated, care should be taken to inquire into the extent to which each form of offence has been practised or indulged, guarding against anything like softening down or mitigation. The object in view is that of leading the penitent to a realisation, as full and complete as possible, of his condition as an offender against the Divine Love ; and further, to a recognition of those particular forms of sin wherein his state as a sinner mainly consists.

The inquiry must be searching and explicit, but not to the extent of pressing for details such as may be offensive in character. Let not the priest fail to exact acknowledgment of the kind of sin, and the degree of sin—the extent to which it has been carried, and its frequency ; whether as an occasional thing or a con-firmed habit ; how far striven against, and to what extent and under what circumstances found irresistible. Let him examine the patient definitely as to the forms which it takes in its lesser developments, and in any approaches to it which may fall short of actual in-dulgence in the sin itself.   Let him ascertain, and point out to the offender, the avenues through which the tempter makes his advances, and which therefore need to be carefully kept in mind and fortified against future attacks.   Insist on his keeping nothing back which may be needful to delineate the sin in question in its full extent.   Remember that your main object is to get at, and open to the sinner's view, the springs and sources of his sin, and to show how these find their development in definite practice, in action and omission. In the majority of cases, perhaps in almost every case with which he is dealing for the first time, the priest will find it necessary to open the patient's eyes to an entirely new view of the character and degree of his sinfulness.   His own view is almost sure to be a super-ficial one, or perhaps even an entirely mistaken one. What he regards as his leading sins may possibly be comparatively slight ones, that is, in comparison with others deeper down, of the extent of which perhaps he has little or no idea.   He may thus have failed entirely to learn the real forms of sin for which he specially needs pardon and cure.   Beware of healing " the hurt of my people slightly."

There are three main aspects under which most forms of sin may be grouped, the first two answering to two leading forms of temperament—

(1) First there is the sin of *self-indulgence* in its various aspects and developments.

This form of tendency is often associated with a character of kindness, even generosity, and especially with dispositions of easy good nature. A person with this type of temperament will be placable, not easily offended, and easily appeased. He will even exhibit a certain capacity for self-denial (so long as it does not touch the true inner springs of his selfishness) for the sake of giving pleasure to others, the motive being the pleasure thus afforded to himself in gratitude or reciprocal good offices. The evil of it consists in the underlying motive of self-pleasing. It may go to the extent of the foulest vice, or excess in any form, depending on the constitution and circumstances. In any case, such a one is a lover of pleasure rather than a lover of God. Dives is a type of this form of sin. "In their lifetime they seek their good things." [1] Such people make this present state their rest, and that rest is in creature comforts. What is their sin ?

It is represented by the second commandment in the First Table and by the seventh in the Second Table (see Rom. i. 25). St. Paul, in the first chapter of the Epistle to the Romans, verses 25 to the end, gives an awful picture of the depths of abomination to which indulgence in this form of sin may lead. But the extent of the sin depends not so much on the grossness of its form as in the degree in which the sinner yields himself to the temptation as it appeals to his particular case ; upon the degree of completeness in which he gives himself up to it, in which, in fact, he forsakes God for the idol. For example, a man who would shudder with horror at the form in which this sin is depicted in the passage to which reference has been made, may, nevertheless, incur guilt as deep in the sight of God by

[1] St. Luke xvi. 25.

his indulgence in what may appear a much less heinous aspect of it, simply because this latter happens to be the only form in which this kind of sin has an attraction for him.

The symptoms of this class of sin will be shown in deflections from duty as well as in positive acts of transgression, and especially in sloth or indisposition for the fulfilment of duty. The priest will form his judgment with reference to the prevalence of this class of sin by careful consideration, and by comparing the various instances of sinful act or omission which the penitent has to confess. He must remember that they are only symptoms, and must make it his effort to trace them to their source. For example, dishonesty, duplicity, *i.e.* untruth in any form, may often be the direct consequences of this form of sin, and the cure of these faults must therefore oftentimes be sought in the work of tracing it out to its source and seeking to apply the remedy there. A test question for this kind of treatment is such a one as this :—

" In what kind of things do you place your feeling of rest ? In what directions do you turn as your source of solace and comfort under care and wear and tear ? "

The opposite of this form of sin—antidote and substitute—is the love of God.

(2) The second form of tendency is that which we might designate as consisting in the spirit of *uncharity*.

Its root is pride. It may be accompanied by a considerable capacity for real self-denial and a fair degree of freedom from tendencies towards indulgence in the natural appetites or in the habit of indulgence. It is active and energetic ; in fact, one of its symptoms is that of contempt for those who are otherwise, for the idle, self-indulgent, sensual. One of its leading symptoms, therefore, is that of a spirit of censoriousness. Its developments are exhibited in a disposition for malice in all its forms and degrees ; it may go to the extent which tempts to murder or the infliction of other injury, or it may simply take the form of permanent resentment. It may exhibit itself in the shape of hasty anger ($\theta\nu\mu\acute{o}\varsigma$) or of settled ill-will ($\grave{o}\rho\gamma\acute{\eta}$). The extent of the sinfulness would not depend so much on the actual degree to which it has been carried, as to that degree and form to which the position and circumstances of the sinner would tempt him to carry it. Hence the impossibility of appraising the degree of sinfulness in any case. The varying constitution of the sinner and the varying forms of temptation as applied to various instances may bring about the result that the sin which is intrinsically identical in two or more instances of its performance may be attended with widely varying degrees of guilt in the perpetrators.

One main characteristic, and at the same time most serious form, in which this class of disposition is manifested is that of the spirit of unforgivingness. This is one of the most obstinate forms of sin ; most difficult to eradicate. It may not lead the sinner to any overt act, or even language expressive of the feeling, but it lies hidden in the heart, making it impossible for the sinner to use the Lord's Prayer with any reality, and hence, of course, for him to obtain pardon for his own sins. The vital necessity for special attention to, and drastic dealing with, this form of sin is manifest from the fact of our Lord's reference to it in this prayer, and also from the corollary which follows this prayer in St. Matthew's version of it, "For if ye forgive men their trespasses, your heavenly

Father will also forgive you. But if ye forgive not men their trespasses, neither will your Father forgive your trespasses." [1]

Men of this class of temperament are generally the staunchest friends, whereas those of the first class are not to be so depended upon. Johnson realised this thoroughly when he said, " I love a good hater " ; yet this is not the true fulfilling of the charge, " Love your enemies. . . . For if ye love them which love you, what reward have ye ? do not even the publicans so ? " [2] The achievement of this state of mind may appear impossible where grievous wrong has been suffered and never repented of ; and, of course, the term " love " is not to be understood in the same sense in which it is ordinarily applied with reference to objects of positive affectionate regard. The " love " which is required in this injunction may be regarded as amounting, in the first place, to the absence of resentment, and in the second place, to that remarkable form of sentiment which Seeley so graphically sets forth in his *Ecce Homo*, and which he designates by the term " enthusiasm of humanity," *i.e.* love for humanity as such.

The stress laid by our Lord on the virtue of philanthropy—treating it as something the existence of which in the character necessarily involved the possession of all other elements of excellence—is no doubt the key-thought to the whole system of Christian ethics. He lays it down as the principle on which the final judgment of mankind at the end of the world will be based : " I was an hungred, and ye gave me meat. . . . Inasmuch as ye have done it unto one of the least of these my brethren, ye have done it unto

[1] St. Matt. vi. 14, 15.   [2] St. Matt. v. 44-46.

me." [1] Seeley speaks of the enthusiasm of humanity as " the passion which can lift a man clean out of all sin whatever." He takes it to be something more than the love of individuals as such, or yet the love of a state or community or race—which would be a passion of the same nature as patriotism—for " The patriot," he says, " is not by any means above the temptation to private injustice or treachery, nor will he become more so when his country is the world." [2] He regards this enthusiasm as " a third kind of love," [3] " not of the race nor of the individual, but of the race *in* the individual ; . . . the love not of all men nor yet of every man, but of *the man* in every man." [4] The true view of this form of love is that which recognises in it the love for the Ideal Man, that is, the Christ in every man. This was one of the great maxims which St. Vincent de Paul set forth as the guiding rules of his own life, namely, that one of looking for the Christ in every man, in his dealings even with the most unresponsive and repulsive members of his charge, and addressing himself to that.

There are certain sins which are common to both classes, and which are to be accounted for by the motives which the priest's knowledge of each class supplies, for example, disobedience to authority, masterfulness, arrogance, deceit, fraud, dishonesty in all its forms. These two classes will branch into innumerable varieties, and will even appear to mingle in the same individual. Some persons seem predisposed to deceitfulness and undue secretiveness, but if the scrutiny be carried to the root of the character in question, such tendencies may generally be traced to one or other of the two fundamental principles, those namely which stand in contrast respectively to the two leading principles of religion, the self-seeking character having for its contrast the love of God, the uncharitable character having for its contrast the love of neighbour.

What is to be aimed at then is a love of man for man apart from any individual claims for love. This may perhaps be taken as a good definition of the modern term "altruism." The highest motive for this is the love of Christ and of all humanity, because Christ is in it, permeates it throughout. Our Lord Himself teaches us that this is the essence of Christianity. Its absence, therefore, must necessarily involve a repudiation of the root principle of Christianity. It is this which constitutes the seriousness of the offence, while at the same time it is one of the most delusive of all forms of sin, because it is free from the grossness which imparts a repellent character to other forms of sin, and even carries with it a spurious aspect of justice, of dealing with others as they deal with you. Very full and careful treatment will therefore be necessary in dealing with this subtle and dangerous form of evil.

It has been said that pride was the root principle underlying this class of sin tendency. The pride here referred to does not indeed include the form of it which is known as vanity, for this rather belongs to the former class, that of self-pleasing. The form of pride which is now in question has for its outcome the tendency to masterfulness, arrogance, harshness on the one hand, and disobedience, insubordination, or lack of consideration for the claims of authority, respect, deference, reverence, on the other. If the first of these two classes may be characterised by the term *selfishness*, the term *self-will* is perhaps the most comprehensive designation of the second.

(3) There is a third class of sin which may be called *Satan-sin*, and may be said to consist in the defiance of God.

It is no doubt the sin against the Holy Ghost, and is that which lies at the root of the Third Commandment, being the sin of direct enmity against God. Profanity, in a sense, may be regarded as a sin under this class, for profanity has its source in anger against God.

The sin against the Holy Ghost calls for special attention, for a large proportion of penitents, if not all, are at one time or another oppressed by the dread of being guilty of this sin, and therefore in a hopeless condition. The case to which our Lord refers in speaking of this sin should be carefully noted.[1] It was after the dawn of conviction began to show itself in the hearts of the observers of His miracle of evicting a dumb spirit, leading them to cry out, " Is not this the son of David ? " The Pharisees at once set themselves to stifle this budding life at its outset ; they ascribed our Lord's miracle to the agency of Satan himself, against whose tyrannous rule it was actually aimed. The sin consisted in the fact that the Pharisees recognised the budding life as true life, and the work of God's Spirit, yet, nevertheless, set themselves in opposition against it from motives of enmity against Christ as its Giver, If the charge had been actuated on their part by mere fanaticism or ignorance it would not have been an act of direct and conscious antagonism to the Holy Spirit. Hence, blasphemy against the Holy Ghost signifies the direct and conscious attempt

[1] St. Matt. xii. 22, 23. *Cp.* St. Mark iii. 22–29.

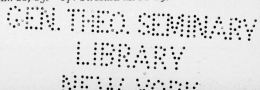

to oppose His influence for the promotion of life in the hearts of others, and is therefore spiritual murder so far as regards the will and effort of the perpetrator. Moreover, to be really guilty of it a man must necessarily have stamped out within himself whatever he had of the Spirit's life or capacity for life ; he must have committed spiritual suicide before he can wilfully attempt spiritual murder—*wilfully*, for a man may even lead others into temptation and sin, and thus bring fearful guilt upon his soul, without yet having reached the condition of one who has wholly abandoned himself to the opposition against God as God, and good as good ; and for him there may be hope. His motive may have been simply that of self-gratification in some form. The penitent who is troubled by fears on this subject may be comforted by the assurance that the very fact of anxiety on the subject is a strong presumption that the Holy Spirit is still striving with his soul, and hence, that the door of hope is still open to him.

It must be remembered that every form of sin has as its natural issue the final result of death—death in its full and ultimate sense—that of utter separation from God. Whatever produces wilful separation of the human will from God's will, or of the human heart from God's love, is soul-destroying, and has death as its goal, the death that means *hell*. [1]

[1] The question, " What is Hell ? " is better left unanswered, except in so far as that it means the horror of great darkness, the disintegration of all the faculties, the misery in all departments of sensation, which must come about when the cosmos of human nature is cast into hopeless and final disorder by permanent separation from God, by Whose loving presence and operation the Order at all points—which is man's normal condition (as love from a physical, and as happiness from a mental point of view)—can alone be maintained. " The worm that never dies " ; " The gnawing of hopeless remorse " ; " The fire that is never quenched " ; or " Passion ever raging, never satisfying " ; " The chains of hamper-

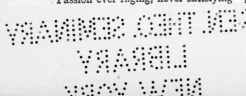

There are different degrees in this condemnation corresponding to differing degrees in glory, " even as one star differeth from another in glory." Sins which have their source merely in passion, in the abuse of natural faculties and dispositions, are, no doubt, as surely fatal to the soul's life as any other form of evil. They incur damnation, yet not so deep and so black as that which represents the condition of the man who has deliberately assumed the position of a satan (an *enemy* to God and good), ranging himself under the standard of the great Satan as fighting in the ranks of Hate against the Love-principle of the cosmos. This latter is, no doubt, the " sin unto death " of which St. John speaks as past praying for (if this is the meaning of the passage 1 St. John v. 16.), *i.e.* sin which has carried the soul to the actual consummation of spiritual death.

We may safely take it as an unquestionable fact that no sin is in itself unpardonable if only the will to

ing constraint " ; are but figures of speech shadowing forth certain features of this awful condition. But be it observed, they are all self-caused, not God-inflicted, and follow as necessary consequences of a course of action of which, in their earlier aspects, they are characteristic features. In those earlier aspects they are attended with a certain measure of what may be called pleasure, and, no doubt, is real pleasure, because not yet divested from the condition of things in which good and evil are mingled. (Pleasure, no doubt, is in its essence good ; as part of the Divine intention for the happiness of His creatures. Its abuse may be a means of gross sin, as, say, the indulgence of our first parents in the forbidden fruit, namely, their selection in defiance of the Divine Will of the time and manner of their participation of that form of good which God's will had reserved for His own.) In their final form, no doubt, the pleasure attending such exercises has vanished, and nothing but horror remains. It is not God Who punishes ; the punishment is self-inflicted, and consists really in the rejection of those benefits which the loving presence of God conveys.

The question why God permits it, or, in other words, permits evil, must remain unanswered while the world lasts. It is not a question with which we are concerned, for the state of perdition is not one which we need incur. The door of salvation is open for us, and for all who are willing to accept the invitation to enter.

repent and turn from it be present. Sin which is characterised as beyond the reach of pardon is only so because the sinner has destroyed within himself the faculty for repentance. Sin against the Holy Ghost then may be said to represent the climax of a course of wilful self-hardening, whereby the will has not only extinguished within itself, deliberately and knowingly, every invitatory impulse which the Holy Spirit lovingly exerts for its salvation, but has definitely placed itself in a position of conscious antagonism to the will of God as such. The reading adopted in the Revised Version for St. Mark iii. 29, " Is guilty of an eternal sin," would seem to represent the true solution of the difficulty often alleged in the idea of an infinite penalty for a finite sin. The fact is that the sentence is eternal only because the sin is eternal, and is actually the natural accompaniment of the sin and not an external punishment. Repentance can never fail in securing pardon.

It may, however, oftentimes be difficult to make sure of the existence of true repentance, of distinguishing true sorrow for sin as such—sorrow which leads the sinner necessarily to turn from his sin, to hate sin as sin and not only as the cause of penalty—from the mere slavish dread of the penalty which is the consequence of sin. It is sometimes as difficult for the sinner as for the priest to make this distinction, to be really sure of the genuineness of his repentance. Many instances of clear self-deceiving in this respect might be adduced from every priest's pastoral experience, instances in which the unreality of the repentance is evinced by the disappearance of the sentiment which stimulated it as soon as the emotion of fear which was its moving cause has been removed. In fact, we may say that the

only safe test of genuineness of repentance is that which
is found in the witness of a changed life in encounter
with temptation. What is known as " death-bed
repentance " must always have an element of uncertainty about it, although, of course, the principle of
hope is always to be encouraged.

The penitent then will, in many cases, need to be
guided in the detection of his besetting sin, and be
taught to follow it up into the various departments of
his life. He must ascertain what special acts of
offence it may have directly or indirectly occasioned.
The object the priest has in view should always be
that of leading the penitent to learn and to keep track
of the working of these tendencies for himself ; the
priest's motive being that of getting the penitent to be,
as soon as possible and as fully as possible, independent
of external priestly ministration. He must learn to
be quick at recognising any deflection from the straight
onward course of duty, from the direction of the
" single eye " fixed on Christ. He is to be guarded
most emphatically against a superficial view of sin.
This is one of the main dangers incident to the spiritual
life. Little instances of forgetfulness or indifference
will often take up in the person's mind the place which
should be occupied by the thought of deeper sins which
they are apt to overlook. In all cases where the sins
confessed are mere peccadillos (and every experienced
priest is aware how frequent such cases are, even among
those in the habit of making confession), it is an unquestionable fact that the penitent is losing sight of
grave and serious sins which sorely need treatment,
and to which it is the priest's business to open the
penitent's eyes. While human nature is what it is,
grave sin must always be present and more or less as

a habit, though it may be striven against and to a great extent kept under. Where there is no sign of this conscious recognition of real, grave sin, and of a steady conflict being carried on against it, the priest may feel assured that serious danger exists, to a sense of which the penitent needs to be aroused.

His object then should be that of training the penitent in self-examination and self-detection, and the priest should not be satisfied until he has led him to a true view of the nature of his own peculiar form of sin, in such a manner as to enable him to enter into and realise that state of feeling on the subject which is expressed in the Confession of the Communion Service. Let him take this as a test of the truth and fulness of the apprehension of his sinfulness in God's sight. When once this condition of true apprehension of sin is attained, and the penitent has learnt to follow out his sin into its various aspects of omission and commission, of thought, word, and deed, and has learnt to gauge his whole conduct unsparingly by this test, he is on the way to fit himself for the higher form of confession, namely, that which is made directly to Christ Himself without the intervention of a human priest.

The investigation into the penitent's position as a sinner having been thus completed, the priest next proceeds to set briefly but distinctly and gently before the penitent a view of the general form and character of the sins which he has confessed, and to instruct him to bring them, as a conscious act on his own part, into the presence of Christ ; and, as it were, lay them down at the foot of the cross.

He must be taught to realise that it is from the sin that he seeks to be free, not the sin's punishment, except in a secondary sense. Hence the necessity of renouncing sin as a definite act. When the penitent has once succeeded in grasping a true sense of his condition as a sinner—a consummation which he may now be supposed to have fairly attained—his part in the sacramental act of confession may be said to have seven stages :—

(1) That of recalling the sin, realising, recognising it as an awful fact.

(2) The experience of sorrow for sin as an offence against the Divine Love. This necessarily implies such a recognition of that Love as involves some degree of responsive love on the penitent's part.

(3) The act of will in renouncing the sin thus recognised, deliberately putting it from him as implied in the work of conversion.

(4) The act of confession proper, submitting the sin for absolution to the great High Priest, laying it before him as it were with a full sense of utter culpability.

(5) The acceptance by an act of faith of the gift of pardon, the gift which, as it were, abolishes the sin, and hence at once conveys to the penitent the blessing of admission to the Divine Love, from which the sin while present had debarred him.

(6) The act of seeking the grace of the Holy Spirit to fortify his soul for its warfare against sin in the future.

(7) The act of setting about the use of that grace ; for, no doubt, the effort to this end must follow instantaneously on the reception of the gift in order to make it effectual.

As has been urged already, the priest must keep before the penitent's view the presence of the Personal

Christ, and remind him of the fact that it is to this Presence that every word and action on his part must be consciously addressed. It may be well, after the view of the penitent's sinfulness has been clearly put before him, that the priest should address to him the question : " Do you now renounce these sins which you now confess ? " and that the penitent should answer : " I renounce them all." Also, after setting before him the view of the great High Priest as the Forgiver of sin, that he should address to him the question : " Dost thou believe in Jesus Christ as thy Redeemer and the Forgiver of thy sins ? " to which it will be enough for him to reply by the simple expression, " I believe." The priest then lays his hand on the penitent's head and pronounces the Absolution as given in the Office for the Visitation of the Sick.

It will generally be found desirable, after the confession of sin has been completed, and before the two questions and answers referred to, that a short prayer or collect should be used asking for grace to approach the coming sacramental gift in the true spirit of penitence and faith. After the Absolution will follow one or two suitable collects, concluding with the twofold form of blessing in the Visitation of the Sick, beginning with the words, " O Saviour of the world."

The almost startling distinctness and positiveness with which the action of Absolution is expressed in the form just referred to has deterred many devout and conscientious priests from its use. And, in fact, the responsibility attending its use may well be regarded as so awful as to make necessary the utmost searching of heart before a man dares to take it into his lips. The peril of contributing towards the perdition of a soul by encouraging it in a condition which falls short of that which is contemplated in the action, is something which may well appear almost too weighty for mortal man to bear. Of course anything like perfection in the qualifications of penitence and faith which the sinner is supposed to bring to the sacrament is out of the question ; but the element of reality and deep sincerity must be present, as well as true comprehension of what is implied in both. Before taking into his lips these awful words the priest must be enabled to assure himself that his part in the matter has been fully and faithfully fulfilled, and that in his conscience he is persuaded that the penitent's part has also been fully and faithfully fulfilled to the best of his capacity.

The spiritual director must bear in mind the necessity of warning the penitent of the dangers attending the reaction which, in the natural course of things, will be likely to follow the strain of devotional effort involved in the exercise in which he has been engaged. The glow of spiritual fervour and exaltation of faith by the consciousness of the unspeakable blessedness of the gift which has been received is a form of emotion which, from its very nature, must be transient. There is danger lest, in the cooling down of the emotion, the good results which it has been the means of stimulation may be suffered to fade and die. In any case, the cooling down of religious emotion gives the adversary the opportunity of which he is never slow to take advantage. No doubt this is one of the great tests of the sincerity and earnestness of the penitent, of the reality of his confession and his acceptance of the absolution. The true test of earnestness, reality in the work of undertaking, consists not in what the man says or does under the influence of excited feeling, but in what he says and does when the excitement has died away, when effort has to be made as it were in cold blood, and often as it might seem against the grain. It may no doubt be said that the most effectual efforts of the spiritual life, and those which bring the greatest blessing, are those which are made under these circumstances, and which are only accomplished by determined opposition to the inclination of the time being. Our Lord's temptation in the wilderness immediately following the outpouring of grace consequent upon the descent of the Holy Spirit upon Him by the waters of Jordan; [1] and again, St. Paul's translation into the third heaven followed by the " thorn in the flesh, a messenger of Satan to buffet " [2] him, are instances evidently intended to warn us of the general rule in spiritual things : *after great grace, great trial.* The penitent therefore needs to be warned at this critical moment to exercise watchfulness at the time of cooling emotion which is certainly at hand ; warned that his sincerity is to be tested, not by his feelings at the present time, but by his actions when the present feeling of fervour has passed away.

The question will naturally be raised as to the length of time which would necessarily be occupied in the process of treatment which has been sketched in the preceding pages, and the writer would take advantage of this opportunity to express his conviction of the necessity of such a prolonged course of treatment, especially in the case of those who are novices in the realities of the spiritual life, if the treatment is to be productive of any permanent effect and is to penetrate into the real depths of the man's inner nature. His experience would teach him that a man cannot be

---

[1] St. Mark i. 9–13a.   [2] 2 Cor. xii. 2–10.

hurried into the possession of spiritual life. The mind must be left to " work out its own salvation with fear and trembling," [1] only guided in so doing by wise and kindly direction ; and can only attain it step by step, each stage of advance being carefully made sure before the next is aimed at. The writer would commend this view most earnestly to the consideration of his younger brethren. His own experience is to the effect that more than one interview, sometimes several, will be found necessary before the confession is satisfactorily completed and the penitent may be regarded as ripe for absolution.

[1] Phil. ii. 12.

THE SICK

I. General

THE sick, for the purpose of spiritual treatment, may generally be divided into four classes as regards their condition of infirmity—

1. The aged or permanently infirm.

2. Sickness of considerable duration, but not permanent.

3. Temporary and not immediately dangerous sickness.

4. Dangerous or mortal sickness, again subdivded into—

> (*a*) Slow and long continued.
> (*b*) Comparatively rapid.
> (*c*) Hurried cases, *e.g.* where the patient has but a few days or hours to live.

In connection with any of these, special treatment may be required for cases in which the powers of the mind are affected, whether by way of exhaustion or aberration.

A different and carefully thought-out method will have to be undertaken in each of these several classes. No extempory or haphazard treatment should be practised. It may be well in each case to have a method drawn out in writing, including subjects of reading and exhortation, prayers, Offices used, and so forth. Of course these will have to be modified by circumstances, and by any peculiarities of character and disposition which the patient may develop. Under the skilful touch of the experienced practitioner the patient may develop conditions of soul entirely novel and unexpected.

With regard to their spiritual condition patients may roughly be divided into five classes—

1. Faithful and devout Church-people.

2. The careless, formal, and indifferent.

3. The manifestly irreligious, Churchmen or otherwise.

4. Dissenters, religiously minded.

5. The sceptical or unbelieving.

It may be difficult to decide into which category his patient is to be assigned, but the pastor must, like the physician, carefully note all the symptoms, taking into consideration whatever knowledge he may possess of his patient's lack of conversion, and form his judgment and regulate his treatment accordingly. The best course will usually be to ascertain the patient's own view of his condition by direct questions, plain and straightforward, yet carefully chosen ; any bluntness or harshness, or anything which is likely to wound the feelings unnecessarily, being carefully avoided. The class to which the patient belongs, and the treatment to be pursued, must at the outset be a matter of careful consideration and prayer for guidance. The pastor must avoid the two opposite forms of error : (1) depending on his own powers, (2) neglecting to exercise those powers to the utmost, as expecting spiritual guidance apart from that exercise. It is said somewhere, "To pray without working is presumption ; to work without praying is atheism." The man who, instead of exercising careful self-preparation, allows himself to approach this duty unprepared has no right to expect that the hurried uplifting of a prayer for help and guidance, at the moment when it is needed, will draw down such spiritual aid as to make up for the deficiency caused by his own laziness and negligence.

As to the length of the visit, *better too short than too long*. Twenty minutes may perhaps as a general rule represent a duration which is sufficient without being too lengthy. In cases of extremity it will often be necessary to cut down the visit to a much shorter period, five minutes being sometimes as long as a patient's condition will bear.

The priest must, of course, make a point of keeping himself in cordial touch with the doctor. Difficulties between the two professions often arise with regard to this matter of sick visitation. Such difficulties, however, as the writer's experience would tend to suggest, are in most cases the consequence of lack of judgment on the part of the clergyman. Whenever he manifests a readiness to place himself in the doctor's hands as regards time, the duration and character of his visits, he will seldom find much serious objection on the part of the latter. In fact, the experienced physician will generally recognise that the ministrations of a wise and gentle clergyman have a beneficial effect in the way of quieting and soothing the patient's nerves, and therefore, even when no one else is admitted to the sick-bed, the priest's visits will be allowed under proper restrictions. In the sick-room the doctor's word is law. The priest may indeed recognise his own rights as guardian of the soul, as the doctor is of the body, but practically speaking, he will not find it feasible to pit himself as a matter of right against the physician of the body.

Hence his only course is to make it a matter of earnest effort to establish and maintain friendly relations and mutual confidence between himself and the doctor.

In cases where the patient's condition is not of that extreme character calling for special brevity on this account, a little general conversation on ordinary topics may be a suitable opening for the visit, and may tend to do away with anything like stiffness or formality.

In proceeding to the really spiritual ministrations it is absolutely necessary to secure the kindly and cordial attention of the patient, to avoid anything which may have the effect of repelling or irritating him. To this end the very greatest patience is requisite. The priest should avoid pressing his exhortations if the patient appear tired or fretful. He should in this case desist with a good grace and in a good humour, and let them stand over for another occasion. He must himself beware of the very slightest loss of temper. At the same time let it be understood that these matters *are standing over*, not abandoned.

It is a matter of great importance that the priest should make a point of seeing the patient alone from time to time, especially in his earlier visits. This is necessary in order that he may come to an understanding with the patient as early as possible, and the attainment of this object must be brought about carefully and deliberately, and in no wise hurried over. Arrangements for his being left alone with the patient should be made with the friends before entering the sick-room, in order that it may be brought about easily and naturally so as to avoid the possibility of disturbing the patient's feelings by making the request in his presence. It will, however, be desirable that friends should be present during a *portion* at any rate of each visit (except in cases of extreme weakness or nervousness), and in general, that the family should be present during a brief office of reading and prayer with which the clergyman will usually close his visit.

In many cases it will be found desirable from time to time for the priest to pray with the patient alone after having attained his confidence as to the needs which the prayer should specially express. The main reason for being often alone with the patient is that of affording opportunities for the reposal of such confidence. The faithful priest will always make it a matter of earnest endeavour and careful thought to invite and draw out this confidence. He must feel that he has not attained his true position as pastor until he has won the patient over to speak freely and confidentially to him. For the attainment of this end he should make it manifest that he regards sin from the standpoint of a fellow-sinner with heartfelt sympathy for the offender, without censoriousness, and at the same time with a deep and awful sense of its ruinous character. If, by reason of the patient's weakness or disinclination, he drops the subject for a while and speaks of other things, he must return to it again at an early opportunity (perhaps his next visit, made as early as possible for the purpose) with gentle firmness, and seek, by a manner expressive of great earnestness coupled with loving sympathy, to overpower the disinclination to approach a subject so tender, which a patient unaccustomed to spiritual things will often manifest.

It is certainly desirable that the pastor should not confine himself to spiritual topics in his conversation with the patient. He will generally find him ready to speak on the subject of his malady ; sometimes also on more general topics : but the pastor must carefully avoid allowing this kind of conversation to take up any considerable portion of the time of his visit, unless indeed he is in the habit of paying visits more frequently than necessary for spiritual intercourse, that is, more than once a day.

As regards the office of prayer to be used, it may be somewhat as follows :—

1. A few introductory words giving the keynote to the exercise that follows.

2. A short reading, followed by some words of definite application.

3. Prayers bearing some reference, if possible, to

    (a) The subject of the reading and exposition.

    (b) The patient's condition and needs.

4. Some closing form of Benediction.

The priest should then take his leave at once, always making the act of worship the last thing, and not allowing its effect to be impaired by subsequent conversation on ordinary topics.

The prayers had better be, in part at any rate, extempore. The great value of sound forms of prayer should be kept before the view of the flock, and emphasised by the pastor's use of them, even though meanwhile he includes the use of extempore prayer as needful to meet certain objects which are not included within the printed forms.

The priest should see that the patient's friends are provided with suitable prayers, and should make it one of his first acts to instruct them in the use of these, and to urge that use upon them. He should also point out portions of Scripture suitable to be read to the sick person.

II. Emergency Cases of Greater or Less Urgency

The priest will naturally provide himself with
forms of offices to suit all classes of cases, from those
with reference to whom time is no object to those
who are in urgent extremity. Some cases may mean
even minutes, when the priest can hardly do more than
point to the cross of Jesus. Even in such a case he
should remember that there are two objects to be
sought : (1) Confession of sin in the heart of the sufferer,
i.e. repentance—the act of turning from sin ; (2) the
act of grasping the personal Jesus Christ as the Saviour
from sin. There must be a realising (1) of sin as sin,
and as separating from God, and (2) of Love, infinite
and perfect, as the bond of union between Saviour
and sinner.

Remember it is not enough, in cases where the
sufferer is conscious, to pray for him ; the act of
renunciation of sin and the act of acceptance of Christ
must be his own, and it is the priest's part to help him
to make it. Even the case of one apparently uncon-
scious is not necessarily to be despaired of in this sense.
It will often be found suitable to address a word or two
to one in this state, such as : " Brother, draw nigh to
God, and He will draw nigh to you." The priest will
in such a case frame his prayer in brief, simple phrases
with perhaps a short interval between each, embodying
what he realises as the actual need of the sufferer in his
present position. Let him thus plead for him, at the
same time wording his prayer in such a manner as to
make it suitable to be the prayer of the sufferer for
himself. It would be well that the priest should
beforehand prepare suitable forms for such an occasion,

in order that there may be no waste of words, no hesitation, no room for regret afterwards at having left out something of importance.

When the time for preparation is longer, but yet only a few days or perhaps weeks in duration, or when the condition of weakness makes it necessary to lay as little strain as possible on the patient's attention and feeling, it is important that the priest should carefully consider what is the minimum in the way of treatment which he is justified in exercising on account of the taxing of the patient's powers. Of course this will vary almost indefinitely in different cases in accordance with the different stages of spiritual condition which the patient may exhibit, as also with the patient's capacity for apprehending spiritual truth.

The actual requirements may perhaps be divided somewhat as follows :—

(1) The love of Christ.

(2) The actual effective presence of Christ, and the love of Christ as we are concerned in it, *i.e.* as shown as a love for sinners.

Hence the patient must be led to realise the fact of his position as a sinner as being the point of touch between him and the love of Christ as the Lamb of God Who takes away sin. And for the attaining of this end his sin must be in some way brought clearly home to him. If his conscience, unaided by external influence, is sufficient to bring about this object, it is well ; but this will be the case only in a small minority of instances. The natural tendency to put sin on one side is one of the most frequent and serious difficulties attending the office of the spiritual director to convince the ordinary patient of this condition of sin.

There is danger, no doubt, of offending and repelling

I

a patient to such an extent as to be fatal to the priest's influence, but there is greater danger of confirming his apathy and impenitence, which is still more fatal. The priest must be loving, gentle, humble, ready to speak of himself as a fellow-sinner, eager to point out to his erring brother the source of peace and deliverance which he has already found for himself. Let the intensity of his earnestness appear in his manner, but let him avoid the smallest approach to harshness or impatience. He must beware of wearying the patient ; physical weariness is oftentimes utterly subversive of spiritual benefit. The priest should if possible avoid carrying his ministrations to the point at which such a condition begins to manifest itself, unless of course time is very pressing and the end very near. He should break off the interview with a kindly, pleasant word the moment he perceives any approach to irritation or impatience on the part of the patient : a watchful eye should be kept on the patient's frame of mind and feeling, and the treatment adapted accordingly.

In the framing of the diagnosis the treatment would, of course, be modified according to the confidence felt as to spiritual attainment on the part of the patient ; but its general principles would be applicable to all. Having thus awakened in the penitent a true consciousness of sin, that is, of his own special and particular sins, the priest now goes on to set before him the duty of repentance ; carefully explaining the difference between that sorrow which is the result of regret for, or dread of, the consequences of sin—and which is only a form of selfishness—and on the other hand, sorrow for the sin itself as being offensive to a loving Father, the root of which sorrow is therefore love. The next step to be enforced is confession—

clear, definite, explicit, special as well as general—to be made by the penitent to Christ as the great High Priest, Who, although He knows all things, requires confession as a condition of forgiveness in order that the penitent may fully realise his own need of such forgiveness. The act of confession must, of course, be accompanied by—

1. An act of contrition.

2. An act of faith, or acceptance of the pardon desired, as effected through the atonement accomplished by the Blood of Christ.

3. An act of resolution, including the abandonment of motives governing the past life, and the adoption of the new motive of love of God for the life which is to follow.

To make these steps effectual the exercise of faith, or the reposal of the trust on the Saviour's willingness and power to grant what is asked, is an essential requirement. The patient, when truly in earnest, will often be found to complain of weakness of faith, or even of absence of faith. He must be assisted by the explanation of the difference between faith and assurance, and reminded of the fact that faith may often be truly present and effectual even though it be hampered and clouded by much of doubt and mental uneasiness. He should be taught that it is an act which he is to perform, that is, an *act* of self-surrender, and not merely a feeling for him to entertain. He should be supported by the declaration that Christ's promise is an absolutely sure thing ; that it applies to his case as much as to that of any other person, and that the only question is whether he is willing to accept it and to yield his whole heart and life in return. Lastly, the penitent must be reminded of the necessity of steady and consistent effort on his own part to carry on the process of grace and " work out his own salvation with fear and trembling," remembering that such a crisis as this calls forth Satan's strongest efforts to counteract the Spirit's influence ; and that on this account special watchfulness, instant prayer, and active effort will be necessary to maintain and carry forward the benefit which has been gained.

In the application of this method of special treatment it is, of course, most necessary to take into consideration the patient's physical condition. The priest must avoid wearying him by remaining with him too long ; he must be careful not to repel him by the slightest note of harshness or severity of manner or tone, not to frighten him by abruptness or by a dictatorial air. With St. Paul, he must be " all things to all men, that by all means he may save some." [1] He is to angle for souls. His whole bearing must be kindly and soothing, avoiding anything like gloom or dismalness of aspect or manner. He must aim at appearing cheering and sunshiny, yet, with all this, his treatment of the patient's soul must be firm and decided, avoiding anything like timidity or false diffidence. He must sum up his manhood, his sense of responsibility, and speak plainly and straight to the point. He will find this method of treatment to be most satisfactory to the patient, as well as most effectual in its results. On first entering upon a case it may not be desirable to proceed abruptly to spiritual matters, but while exercising his judgment in this matter as to what other topics he shall touch upon, he must be careful not to waste time and the patient's strength should the patient be very weak and unfit for much talk or thought.

[1] I Cor. ix. 22b.

A frequent fault in pastoral visits is that they are too long. A visit is better too short than too long. It is absolutely essential that the clerical visit should be regarded by the patient as something pleasant and desirable. It may sometimes appear difficult to reconcile the attainment of this object with that degree of faithfulness and effective spiritual treatment which is the main object of all pastoral ministration, and possibly there are times when the condition of the patient's mind may render it impossible to make the visit an agreeable and pleasant thing in his eyes. But this unsatisfactory frame of mind may generally be avoided by (1) kindly and affectionate gentleness on the priest's part, and (2) the manifestation of profound earnestness and eager interest in the patient's spiritual welfare. Those two sentiments evidenced by the priest's manner towards the patient will generally be found irresistible in winning his good will and securing a welcome on his part for the priest's presence. Supposing a visit to be necessarily unwelcome in its character, it should be made as brief as possible in its duration, and there should be an effort to close it with some expression of kindly and affectionate interest such as might win the patient's good will for the next visit, time having elapsed for the present feeling of irritation to pass away. It is most important that the priest and the penitent should always part at the close of such a visit in a spirit of cordiality on both sides.

One great secret of success in making his presence welcome and pleasing to his patient is that of a cheerful manner. Carefully avoiding anything like levity, an air of quiet cheerfulness, even brightness, of manner should always be aimed at. A gloomy manner, even without harshness, is always repellent. The writer can never forget an instance which was brought to his notice in his earlier years. A parishioner of his own, a man who had lived a worldly life, was suddenly stricken down by erysipelas whilst on a visit in the course of business to a distant city. The clergyman of the parish, an earnest, faithful man, was sent for to visit him. The wife of the sick—and as it turned out, dying—man described with indignation the manner in which he had made his approach to the patient. " Mr. ——," he said, in a loud, harsh voice, " is your soul saved ? " The sick man turned his face to the wall and refused to listen to, or accept any effort of ministration from, the clergyman whose presence in the first instance he had desired. And so he died.

Cases of such glaringly injudicious conduct would no doubt be rare, still there is need of constant watchfulness to guard against even slighter approach to undue severity of manner : *suaviter in modo fortiter in re* (gently in manner, strongly in matter) is a safe motto for clerical conduct. The attitude of feeling the spiritual as well as the physical pulse, metaphorically speaking, is one of the great secrets of success in this branch of work ; and the main secret in attaining this attitude is the cultivation of personal love towards the patient. Remember that love is a thing to be cultivated, and not only and solely spontaneous in its production.

Sin, then, is to be viewed, and brought before the patient's view, in its relation to the love of Christ Who bore sin, and the Blood of Christ, the outcome of that love, which takes away sin. The priest must avoid the common error of practically appearing to do all for the patient, while the patient merely watches him do it. His work is a failure until he has led the patient distinctly to undertake two acts for himself: (1) renunciation of sin, (2) grasp upon Christ. For both, of course, the Spirit's power is necessary and must be sought for accordingly by the priest for the patient, and by the patient for himself. The capability for setting these fundamental truths in a plain and practical manner before the penitent, and of moving and assisting him to act upon them, must necessarily call for diligent and careful planning and preparation in the solitude of the study. To relegate it to the spur of the moment is sinful remissness which can hardly escape failure.

The above-stated view is, of course, that of the fundamental aspect of the object to be sought. But the objective point to be aimed at in the treatment of the patient must always be the Sacrament of the Holy Communion, not as an end in itself, but as a means of supplying the end, recognition of which and the longing for its supply have already been awakened.

It cannot be too often insisted upon that the object to be kept in view is the love of Christ, rather than the dread of judgment. At the same time, due stress must be laid upon the fact of Christ's awful purity which makes the contact of sin intolerable to Him, though not the contact of the sinner longing to be freed from it. The case of the leper in St. Mark i. 40 may be taken as representing the ideal view of the approach of the sinner to Christ : " If Thou art willing, Thou art able to cleanse me." The reference is not to deliverance from the consequences of sin, but to the cleansing from sin itself, and the recognition of the fact of that cleansing as following necessarily on the touch of Christ's personality—" Jesus put forth His hand and touched him." The personal apprehension of the personal, loving, present Jesus, listening, speaking, touching, is the only effective presentment which will prevail upon the penitent in his work of conversion.

A very important point is the aspect of Christ to be set before the penitent. It is possible that he will simply view Him as a mere invisible man, differing from any ordinary human being only in the fact of being invisible and of being specially powerful and specially kind. This inadequate view must be guarded against. It is Jesus as *God as well as man* Who must be set before the eyes of the penitent, and Who must be kept in view as the ultimate Object of his love and trust and obedience, as well as the Father as Father. It is true that the presentment of Christ may come first—he who sees Him sees the Father [1]—but this should be only a stepping-stone to the view of the Father as Father. The penitent must learn to approach the Father's presence as brought to it by the Son, the barrier between the sinner and the Father being removed by the Father's acceptance of the Son's blood-shedding. "I go to My Father and your Father" [2] is amongst our Lord's parting words. The Father is ours because His. He is the Only-Begotten, the Only Son. We are sons simply through our share in the single sonship of the Only-Begotten, because through the Incarnation we are made one with Him, so that His life is our life, His sonship our sonship. The Latin term "adoption," so often used to distinguish our relation to the Father from that of the Only-Begotten Son, is altogether misleading, as implying a fiction. The Greek term υἱοθεσία [3] is capable of a much deeper sense, that of our transference to the actual condition of sonship, not a mere supposition of such relationship.

---

[1] St. John xiv. 9b.   [2] St. John xx. 17.
[3] Eph. i. 5 ; Gal. iv. 5 ; Rom. viii. 15, 23 ; ix. 14.

The sinner must learn to approach the Father for himself, at the same time holding fast to the Mediator Who has taken him into union with Himself, and Who is the means of extending the Father's love to Himself as Son so as to make it the possession of the sinner who has become one with Him by His Incarnation, made individually effective by the use of sacraments. The Holy Spirit must, of course, be kept in view for His work's sake. The aid of His energetic operation is requested for the purpose of enabling the penitent to turn to due account the means of the approach to the Father through the Son in which his salvation consists. Such collects as that for the Nineteenth Sunday after Trinity and that at the beginning of the Communion Service are amongst the most suitable for this purpose.

III. THE USE OF THE VISITATION OFFICE

There are probably few clergymen who have not been conscious of a sense of disappointment on first taking up this Office, even while recognising the fact that the acts of worship of which it consists are, as regarded in themselves, most beautiful and suitable. The disappointment arises from the fact that it lacks any distinct act of supplication for the patient's relief from his present sickness and restoration to health. With the exception of the phrases " assuage his pain " and (with reference to a sick child) " deliver him in Thy good appointed time from his bodily pain," we have no definite prayer for bodily relief or recovery.[1] Ancient offices on this subject were well provided

---

[1] This was written before the revision of the Canadian B.C.P.—ED.

with acts of intercession of this sort. The following beautiful prayer is founded on the Greek :—

" O Lord our God, Who curedst by a word alone terrible and deeply rooted diseases, and didst heal a fever of the mother-in-law of Peter ; do Thou, O Lord, now also heal this Thy servant of the plague which afflicts him, Thou Who chastenest in compassion and healest in mercy, Thou who canst remove all disease and weakness, raise him from a bed of sickness and a couch of suffering, laying upon him the balm of Thy mercy.[1] Grant him perfect health and soundness, for Thou art the Healer of our souls and bodies. To Thee we ascribe glory, Father, Son and Holy Spirit, now, always, and for ever and ever. Amen."

The Gospel used in connection with this prayer is St. Mark v. 24–34, the healing of the woman with the issue.

This deficiency in the matter of direct and definite supplication for removal from bodily sickness and

[1] " Laying on him the balm of Thy mercy "—there may not be any actual reference in this expression to the practice of anointing the sick, though it looks somewhat like it. The question, however, of the observance of this sacramental ordinance is being revived at the present time, and it will probably pass into general use in the near future. This is not the place for discussing the general subject, but it is the writer's opinion that its use may be found most helpful in consideration of the fact that the Church has the deepest interest and responsibility in the welfare of the bodies, as well as the souls, of its members. And the analogy of our Saviour's own practice and that of His Apostles, together with the charge expressed in the oft-cited passage in St. James (v. 14, 15), would seem likely to imply the Church's duty in taking her part in working for the welfare of the bodies as well as the souls of her children. It is not a miraculous cure that is sought, or one directly effected by the agency of prayer irrespective of external means ; it is rather an act of invoking a blessing on the use of those means, and of appealing for their salutary effect. The sacramental use of the outward and visible sign thus prescribed will no doubt be most helpful in stimulating the faithful recipient at a moment when, owing to physical weakness, he may be expected to stand in most extreme need of such assistance.

restoration to bodily health is a very serious one, and if, as is generally suggested, our present Office be taken as a model on which to found our method of ministration, in this branch of its application it will be necessary for the priest, in this respect, to deviate widely from the example here set before him. Prayer, clear, definite and explicit, for succour in bodily need must form a conspicuous feature in ministrations of this kind.

It is most essential that a sick person should be brought to converse with the pastor easily and freely, and not that he should merely listen to reading, exhortation, and prayer. The priest cannot feel that he has made any satisfactory progress in the work of dealing with his patient until he has succeeded in leading him to open his heart as to his spiritual condition. In many cases there will be difficulty in bringing this about. The utmost gentleness as well as firmness and unconquerable patience will be necessary. The patient's reserve of diffidence should be overcome by drawing him into the expression of feeling or opinion, not necessarily at first in direct reference to his own case, then gently drawing him into saying something about himself. The main secret consists in the manifestation of heartfelt interest on the priest's part in everything concerning the welfare, whether spiritual or temporal, of the patient.

A great help towards giving point and purpose to instruction and exhortation, and also towards drawing forth the confidence of the patient, will be found in making the Holy Communion—the preparation for it, and the blessings attached to it—a leading subject of consideration. This should in fact, in the case of serious or prolonged sickness, after the diagnosis has once been determined, be made the principal topic

towards which the patient's attention is directed. Of
course this subject, the Holy Communion, is only
applicable to baptised members of the Church. It may
be said that the subject of the Holy Communion to
our own people, and baptism or confirmation to out-
siders, will be the key to the regulation of all sorts of
spiritual intercourse ; and this as a goal in each case
—that is, an embodiment of the means for the attainment of the object to be ever kept in view—the love
of Christ in its constraining effect upon the love of the
member of Christ. The method of preparation and
the qualifications exacted must indeed vary according
to the patient's capabilities and the character of the
case, its urgency, and the probable duration of the
sickness. The priest, like his Master, must judge a man
" according to what he hath," and not " according to
what he hath not." [1] He must in each case consider
how " much has been given " in the way of light and
capability, and then judge how " much will be
required." [2] Where there is a sufficiency of time, full
and careful preparation should be made if present
readiness is lacking. One form of error, which is very
generally prevalent, to be carefully avoided is that of
endeavouring to teach the patient too much at a time,
or to carry him along too rapidly. Even in the case of
the most intelligent, the priest must be prepared for
what will seem to him a considerable degree of obtuse-
ness on the part of his learner. He must therefore be
careful to make sure, by conversation, that each step
of the instruction he is endeavouring to impart is
followed and apprehended by the patient. Hence it
is always better to limit the instruction to matters
absolutely essential. In any case he should satisfy

[1] 2 Cor. viii. 12.　　　　　[2] St. Luke xii. 48.

himself that the patient has attained the following
requisites :—

1. A consciousness of sin, definite and specific, in
himself personally.

> (a) As a condition of general ruin and disorder.
> (b) As exhibited in definite acts of trans-
> gression.

2. Sorrow for sin, as an outrage against the love
of a Father.

3. Confession of sin, both general and particular.
(The question whether this should be through the
human priest, or to the Saviour alone, is one to be
settled according to the priest's best judgment.)

4. Renunciation of sin as accompanying the act of
confession.

5. The possession of faith, that is, faith in general
such as consists of belief in the facts of the Christian
system. (For this purpose the interrogatory form of
the Creed is most suitable, with expansion—and possibly
pauses for audible answers—if the priest thinks
necessary.)

The priest must take particular care in the matter
of the examination, as also of exhortation or consolation, lest the patient should be inclined to listen to
these with a general sense of vagueness and lack of
definite application. He must avoid the condemnation of crying " Peace, peace, when there is no peace." [1]
Many souls have certainly suffered, it may be perhaps
shipwreck, from their hurts thus being healed slightly.
The patient will generally be satisfied with the vague
and indecisive method of treatment referred to, at all
events, will *appear* to be satisfied ; for there can be
no doubt that many, under these circumstances, are

[1] Jer. viii. 11.

conscious of needs and desires which this superficial treatment does not reach, and which, through diffidence or reserve, they are led to repress. In some instances this lack of faithfulness on the part of the priest is followed by the melancholy (for the Church's credit) result that the patient will open his grief to some other adviser with whom he feels more at ease, or whose greater plainness of speaking has succeeded in extracting those expressions of fear, desire, or aspiration, which the pastor has failed to elicit. Many are lost to the Church and gained to Dissent in this way. Whatever may be the reason, it is certain that conversation on directly spiritual subjects is more usual among Dissenters than among Church-people; to our shame be it spoken.

Great plainness and directness of speech, therefore, is amongst the first requisites for profitable visitation of the sick. It must, however, be chastened by sympathetic tenderness and gentleness, for no doubt some have been lost to the Church through harshness and abruptness, what may be called " clumsiness " in the priest's method of dealing with them.

As in the treatment of physical disease, each case will call for its separate method of dealing. A pastor's first duty, therefore, on undertaking a case of spiritual visitation, is to make a diagnosis of it on the same principle as though it were one of physical disease. He must first carefully note and combine the symptoms as they are presented to his view, partly by inquiry, partly from observation, and partly from his previous knowledge of the person. Any inquiries which he may make must, of course, be carefully and cautiously conducted; that is, in such a manner as not to repel or irritate. It is generally desirable to seek some sort

of information as regards the patient's spiritual state
from his friends, say parents or husband, but in so
doing he must guard against what may appear intrusive
or impertinent ; good taste must be his guide. His
method of inquiry must vary according to the patient's
position in life, habits, education, and so forth. The
poor will accept and expect much more direct and
paternal treatment than those in what are termed the
" upper " classes. Priests are warned to be " wise
as serpents " [1] to entrap souls, using various kinds of
" bait," of " play," to land different kinds of fish.

The priest will find a great secret for success in the
practice of keeping plainly before his own eye, and the
eyes of all concerned, his position of responsibility
and authority which gives him the right of interposition—such as belongs to no other relation of life—in
the spiritual instruction of those under his charge.
Yet this assertion of responsibility and authority must
be carefully guarded against any appearance of self-
assertion. His attitude, so far as regards his own
personality, must be one of humility, gentleness, and
unfailing kindliness. Remember that you have to lead
the patient not merely to place himself in your hands
(as in the Roman system) for you to manage the work
of his salvation, but that you have rather to lead him
to " work out his own salvation in fear and trembling,"
the Holy Spirit working in him " both to will and
to do." [2]

The priest must carefully ascertain the patient's
own view of his spiritual condition, and, knowing how
liable human nature is to ruinous error on this point,
his manifest duty is to set before him clearly and fully
the tests on which his act of self-judgment should be

[1] St. Matt. x. 16.   [2] Phil. ii. 13.

founded. He must especially guard him against the false peace which is expressed in such assertions as : " I know that I have sinned ; but I am not worse than others " ; " I trust in God's mercy, and I hope that all will be well in the end." The duty of self-examination must be clearly explained and strictly enforced.

The question as to how far the priest is justified in seeking an explicit confession of sin from the sick member is a difficult one ; in deciding it the strong prejudice on this subject which is generally current among Church-people must be taken into consideration. The Rubric in the Visitation Service seems to direct that the priest should not insist upon any such confession unless he perceives, or has strong reason to believe, that the patient has that on his conscience which will render its quieting impossible by any other means. It is under such circumstances as we are now considering that the priest's possession of that principle of *tact*—which is one of the most radically essential of all his qualifications for the satisfactory fulfilment of his official duties—may be effectually tested. It will seldom be found difficult to elicit such a degree of confidential acknowledgment on the part of the patient as may suffice for all essential purposes, without exciting the ever-ready suspicion of sacerdotalism, if only the priest be capable of exercising wise judgment in his manner of dealing with him. It may often be found the best course to enumerate the various forms of sin one after another, giving sins of omission their due place, touching with gentle and firm hand those sins of the flesh from the acknowledgment of which men usually shrink most of all. This enumeration should expressly be made for the purpose of aiding the patient in self-examination, and may well be put in the form of questions with a pause at the close of each inquiry, and the patient be invited to answer each one silently in his own heart to God, if not audibly to his pastor. Such treatment will not only conduce towards the patient's self-acknowledgment, and hence self-conviction, but will often have the effect of disposing him, either then and there, or later, to acts of confession to the priest as suggested in the Prayer Book.

The priest should beware of allowing in himself any false diffidence in accepting, and indeed urging, the direct confidence of his people on such occasions, remembering the unspeakable benefit, if not absolute necessity, of free and unrestrained intercourse between penitent and pastor on the subject of spiritual difficulties, and above all on that of the crowning difficulty, namely, sin. He should be on the alert to watch for the smallest indication of desire on the part of the patient to communicate to the priest any expression of spiritual feeling. Care must be taken, however, to avoid any possible substitution of this explicit confession to the priest for the direct and personal confession to Christ, and committal of sin to Him, as made consciously by the sinner. This must be kept clearly before his view, Christ the true Confessor, the true Absolver. Hence the main object aimed at in seeking a confession of sin from the sinner should be that of leading him to bring his sin not so much to the priest as to Christ Himself, to commit it directly to Him, and seek from Him the pardon for the past and the grace for the future. Otherwise there is danger lest the priest suffer himself to be intruded into that position of mediator which belongs to Christ Himself, a procedure which has been the cause of fatal error in the Church. Yet, on the other hand, it is most important that the

K

priest should win the perfect confidence of the patient, and should invite and encourage it, and in many cases urge it, with all his power. Thus it is most important that the patient should clearly understand that his confidence will be fully respected, that what he may say under this seal of confidence will never be repeated without his consent.

The frame of mind which the clergyman will find most generally prevalent amongst those who have lived a worldly and unspiritual life is not that of terror, or even uneasiness, in the prospect of death, but rather that of apathy and indifference. Such persons will readily listen to his words of exhortation and admonition, to the reading of the Scriptures and to the prayers he may offer on their behalf ; yet he will find as a general rule that such acts of ministration, although they may evidently be attended with a soothing and cheering effect on the mind (probably from the impression, however vague and uncertain, that something spiritual is being done for the hearer), nevertheless will have little or no effect in promoting any actual result of good to the sick person. Such result can only be brought about, humanly speaking, by leaving the patient to express himself freely to his director on the subject of his spiritual condition. Hence the necessity of endeavouring to lead him, by such means as have been suggested above, to a definite consciousness of sin, and especially of his own particular and personal sins.

Should the priest always accept the request to receive a definite act of confession ? He certainly should do so when once he feels himself to have acquired the necessary knowledge and experience, for it by no means follows that he possesses such knowledge and experience simply because he is a priest. He should bear in mind especially the case of those who stand in actual need of personal direction, young men or lads and, more particularly, converts from Romanism who have been accustomed to personal guidance and nurture.[1]

If the priest should find difficulty, from the shyness or reserve of the patient, in deciding in what way he may enter upon subjects of this character, he will often find the topic of the Holy Communion an excellent means for introducing a conversation which may bring about the result sought for. He would naturally ask whether the patient was desirous of receiving the Sacrament, at the same time setting forth its special benefits for one in his condition ; and, whether his answer should be in the affirmative or negative, or simply expressive of doubt and uncertainty, the priest would certainly find in it an opening for the introduction of the subject so needful at this stage.

In the case of those who are manifestly strangers to the religious life, it is absolutely necessary to ascertain that the patient is seriously in earnest as regards undertaking a new life. When this has been ascertained, some kind of mental retrospect (proportionate to physical strength and intellectual capacity) over his whole past life should be gently urged upon him ; also an effort at self-examination which may place clearly before him a view of his leading sins and habits of sin. Unless this is done, the apathy produced by a protracted course of irreligion or indifference to religion will blind his eyes to his sins, and his confession will be simply that of the sinfulness of the race rather than the sins of an individual. The priest needs to bear in mind the dreadful possibility of confirming a sinner in his unrepentant condition by acquiescing in an act

[1] See also notes on Auricular Confession, p. 66.

of worship and devotion which is merely formal and utterly unreal. In many cases, especially those of the most ignorant, specific questions will be found absolutely necessary to convey the true recognition of sin. It is probably on this particular point that the success of our Church as a saving institution mainly depends, and on which its failure hitherto (in so far as there has been failure) has been chiefly owing. We are afraid of pressing individual confession in its completeness as a sacramental act, whilst on the other hand, we are hardly provided with anything to serve as an adequate substitute—I mean, anything that is direct, systematic, exhaustive, habitual.[1]   To the lack of this, probably, is due in great measure the deficiency of spirituality so often lamented in our Church. Of course regard must be paid to cases in which such questions will only repel the patient owing to prejudice or suspicion of Romanising methods. In such cases his confidence should be invited by the manifestation of very deep and sympathetic interest in his spiritual condition, and care should be taken to avoid such terms and expressions as would naturally be associated in the patient's mind with Romanism or ritualism. It may even be found desirable in some cases, as has already been suggested, to put the questions without insisting on an audible answer, the patient being urged to make his confession to our Lord in the secrecy of his heart, under each head, a pause being left for him to do so. The Absolution in the Visitation Office is directed to be used only if the patient " humbly and heartily desire it," and then only after " a special confession of his sins." [2]   The priest must ascertain whether the

[1] See also notes on Sacramental Confession, p. 72 bb.
[2] B.C.P. Rubric.   See also section on Sacramental Confession.

desire exists, and must make himself perfectly sure of
the patient's repentance and faith. It is clear that the
Absolution should never be used except after a full and
explicit confession to be conducted in accordance with
the priest's own judgment. He must assure himself
of its completeness by such questions as may seem to
him necessary for the purpose. The frequency with
which clinical Communion should be celebrated must
vary according to the patient's habitual practice in
this respect, his own sense of need and desire for it,
the priest's own judgment in the matter, and the
probable duration of the sickness ; but it should
certainly be, if possible, at regular intervals.

IV. Infectious Diseases

Should the clergyman visit all infectious cases ?
Yes, certainly ; even those of young children where
his instructions and consolation are not needed, and
of persons in a state of unconsciousness or delirium.
It is most important that the priest should not
exhibit any timidity or dread of infection on his
own account or that of his own family. True he may
have a family at home, yet let him remember that
although celibacy is not required by the Church of
England of her clergy, it is not meet that this relaxa-
tion should be suffered to become a hindrance to their
usefulness, and thereby place them in an inferior position
as regards readiness for work to that occupied by our
Roman brethren. As taught in our Saviour's answer
to the man who asked leave of absence to bury his
father, family ties must be disregarded when duty to
the Church is in question on the other side.[1] The
least sign of shrinking from the bedside of a sufferer,

[1] St. Luke ix. 60.

from personal motives, produces an impression on the minds of the sufferer and his friends more unfavourable than he who exhibits such a sign can have any idea of. He may not take encouragement from the acquiescence of the sufferer and his friends, for this will in most cases be given without question.   He must beware of allowing unfavourable comparisons to be drawn between his conduct and that, for example, of the doctor.   Let him feel that his place is where his Master's was, that is, wherever sorrow and suffering are, and let him go there fearlessly, commending himself to his Master's care.   Yet, on the other hand, it is not only the part of prudence, but of imperative duty, to take every precaution against contracting infection himself or imparting it to others.   He has no right to expect special or miraculous exemption from the dangers which others would incur under the same circumstances.   He may not allow himself in that presumptuous idea—which some clergy have been known to express—that he bears, as it were, a charmed life while in the fulfilment of his duty.   To expose oneself rashly or wilfully and unnecessarily to danger must always be regarded as directly sinful.   The priest should therefore inform himself as to suitable disinfectants.   He should take care not to inhale the patient's breath, and should take precaution against carrying away in his clothes particles which may be germs of disease.   His best plan is to have a special coat for the visitation of infectious diseases ; after every such visit he should go straight home before entering any non-infected house ; he should remove his coat outside, shake and brush it well, and then hang it up in the open air.   Of course his next action would be to wash his face, head, and hands thoroughly.

ON THE NECESSITY OF CARE IN PRE-PARING FOR THE RECEPTION OF THE HOLY COMMUNION BY THE PATIENT

MENTION has been made of the Holy Communion as the objective point to be aimed at, so far as regards external observance, in the process of dealing with a soul which needs pastoral care. At the same time, great care and caution will be found necessary to guard the learner against approaching the Sacrament without due preparation and qualification. A man may be in the practice of observing this, and other means of grace, without actual hypocrisy ; he may experience a certain degree of pleasure and satisfaction in the observance ; he may be regular in his prayers and in the performance of other religious duties ; he may appear to himself sincere in his prayers and to a certain extent earnest in their utterance ; his life may be free from gross or flagrant sin—yet, nevertheless, he may be entirely devoid of what may be called real grace : and this because his heart and life have never been completely given up to God, self in some form or other being the ruling principle of his character, and showing itself to his conscience at every turn of his life *as* the ruling principle. Such a man will always carry about with him an underlying suspicion that all is not right with him, that his religion consists merely in external form and observance. He will probably, if he set about the work of self-examination, find himself to be living in the allowed commission of some form of habitual sin. His life has no real conflict in it, or if such a thing should occur at all, it is merely occasional, and the real victory is always gained by the power of evil, that is, self.

Dealing with a case of this kind calls for the very utmost degree of skill on the part of a spiritual director. There is terrible danger of confirming the soul in a condition which is on the way to become ruinous. The priest, then, is to be on the look out for this subtle form of spiritual evil, that, namely, of mere formalism. It may appear to some persons a monstrous thing to say, yet nevertheless it is none the less true, that in many cases there is danger in too frequent Communions. Not that Communion can of itself be too frequent, even daily Communion, but it may be too frequent for the spiritual attainment of the observer. Frequency in Communion calls for a high degree of spiritual attainment, spiritual energy and devotion, or it may be a positive source of injury by degenerating into mere formalism. "Let a man test himself, and so let him eat of that bread and drink of that cup." [1] Clergy have been known to urge a man to come to Communion with a view to acquiring that, without the possession of which he ought not to come at all. Communion is meant to feed and sustain those who are in a state of grace, not to convert men to that state.

It is the fashion nowadays to speak of redemption as though it represented merely deliverance from sin itself, and not from the penal consequences of sin, as though when the sin was forgiven those consequences

[1] I Cor. xi. 28.

must still hold on their way unchanged. This surely is an error. The consequence of sin is *death*—death in its various aspects and stages of moral and spiritual disintegration—the dissolution of that Order which is Heaven's first law. No doubt there are certain consequences which follow the commission of sin in any case, and which are not averted by repentance and absolution ; but those consequences are not to be regarded as penal; they are simply permitted as remedial, disciplinary in their character, wholesome " chastening " which " yields the peaceable fruit of righteousness in them that are exercised thereby " : in those, that is, who " endure " it *as* chastening, in accordance with the pleasantly expressed charge in the Visitation of the Sick : "Take therefore in good part the chastisement of the Lord." We may believe, then, that in the case of true repentance the consequences of sin—in so far as they are attended with suffering— follow naturally to such an extent as they are necessary for the prosecution of the course of discipline which is requisite for the soul's health. It must frequently be the case that while such results of past sin may for one person be a means of salutary discipline, and have the effect of raising him to a higher level of spiritual attainment and growth in grace, to another individual circumstances of similar or practically identical character following as consequences of past sin may form a stage in his downward career, confirming his condition of alienation from the love of God. In one case such consequences become " a savour of life unto life " ; in the other, " a savour of death unto death." [1] The actual consequences of sin as sin must be unspeakably more serious than these temporal accessories which

[1] 2 Cor. ii. 16.

are merely incidental. You will sometimes hear a penitent say with regard to such temporary ills, " God is punishing me for my sins, and I must bear it, for I know I deserve it." He should be taught that the visitations to which he refers have a much deeper significance and wider purpose than he as yet realises. They are to be exhibited and utilised, turned to their due account in the way of promoting the work of correcting his tendencies to sin, and aiding his growth in grace and knowledge.

PRINTED BY
WILLIAM CLOWES AND SONS, LIMITED,
LONDON AND BECCLES.

STANDARD THEOLOGICAL WORKS

PUBLISHED BY THE

SOCIETY FOR PROMOTING CHRISTIAN KNOWLEDGE

London—*S.P.C.K. House,* Northumberland Avenue, W.C.2

New York—The Macmillan Company.

Toronto—The Macmillan Company of Canada.

TRANSLATIONS OF CHRISTIAN LITERATURE

Over 50 volumes of this important Series have now appeared.

TRANSLATIONS OF EARLY DOCUMENTS

A Series of texts important for the study of Christian origins. Under the Joint Editorship of the Rev. W. O. E. OESTERLEY, D.D., and the Rev. Canon G. H. BOX, M.A., D.D.

Twenty-four volumes of this Series have now appeared. "The Book of Enoch" is the best known of the documents, but all deserve the attention of students.

HELPS FOR STUDENTS OF HISTORY

Edited by C. JOHNSON, M.A., H. W. V. TEMPERLEY, M.A., and J. P. WHITNEY D.D., D.C.L.

TEXTS FOR STUDENTS

Little paper covered books costing from 3d. upwards, many with a special appeal to Theologians.

Detailed lists may be had, post free, on application.

ADENEY, Rev. J. H., M.A., Missionary to the Jews in Roumania.

THE JEWS OF EASTERN EUROPE. With four Illustrations. 3s. 6d.

ARNOLD-FORSTER, FRANCES, S.Th.

THE HYMN-BOOK OF THE CHURCH; or, THE GROWTH OF THE PSALTER. 8s.

BARRY, G. D., B.D.

THE INSPIRATION AND AUTHORITY OF HOLY SCRIPTURE. A Study in the literature of the first five centuries. 4s. 6d.

BELL, Rev. G. K. A., M.A. (Editor).

THE MEANING OF THE CREED. Papers on the Apostles' Creed. 7s. 6d.

BENSON, Edwin, B.A.

LIFE IN A MEDIÆVAL CITY ILLUSTRATED BY YORK IN THE FIFTEENTH CENTURY. With eight Illustrations. Paper, 4s.; cloth, 5s.

BIRKBECK, W. J., M.A., F.S.A.

BIRKBECK AND THE RUSSIAN CHURCH. Essays and Articles collected and edited by his friend, ATHELSTAN RILEY, M.A. With Portrait. 8s. 6d.

BROWNE, The Right Rev. G. F., D.D., formerly Bishop of Stepney and of Bristol.

THE VENERABLE BEDE. His Life and Writings. With Illustrations. 10s.

KING ALFRED'S BOOKS. Cloth boards. 30s.

THE IMPORTANCE OF WOMEN IN ANGLO-SAXON TIMES; THE CULTUS OF ST. PETER AND ST. PAUL, and other addresses. With two Illustrations. 7s. 6d.

CARPENTER, S. C., M.A., Fellow and Tutor of Selwyn College, Cambridge.

CHRISTIANITY ACCORDING TO ST. LUKE. 10s. 6d.

CARRINGTON, Philip, B.A.

CHRISTIAN APOLOGETICS OF THE SECOND CENTURY. 7s. 6d.

CUTTS, The late Rev. E. L., D.D.

TURNING POINTS OF ENGLISH CHURCH HISTORY. 3s. 6d.

TURNING POINTS OF GENERAL CHURCH HISTORY. 3s. 6d.

PARISH PRIESTS AND THEIR PEOPLE IN THE MIDDLE AGES IN ENGLAND. With numerous Illustrations. 7s. 6d.

DARRAGH, Rev. John T., D.D.

THE RESURRECTION OF THE FLESH. 18s.

DUCHESNE, Monsignore L.

CHRISTIAN WORSHIP. ITS ORIGIN AND EVOLUTION. A Study of the Latin Liturgy up to the Time of Charlemagne. Translated by M. L. McClure. Fifth Edition. 15s.

ELLIS, Harold, B.A.

CONFIRMATION INTERVIEWS. 7s. 6d.

FERRAR, W. John, M.A.

THE EARLY CHRISTIAN BOOKS. A short introduction to Christian Literature to the middle of the second century. 3s. 6d.

THE UNCANONICAL JEWISH BOOKS. A short Introduction to the Apocrypha and the Jewish Writings 200 B.C. to A.D. 100. 3s. 6d.

FIELD, John Edward, M.A.

THE ENGLISH LITURGIES OF 1549 AND 1661 COMPARED WITH EACH OTHER AND WITH THE ANCIENT LITURGIES. 12s. 6d.

FLETCHER, J. S., Member of the Yorkshire Archæological Society.

THE CISTERCIANS IN YORKSHIRE. With Seven Illustrations by Warwick Goble, and a facsimile from the Chronicles of Meaux. 17s. 6d.

FOXELL, W. J., M.A.

THE TEMPTATION OF JESUS. A Study. 6s. 6d.

GEDEN, Rev. A. S., D.D.

COMPARATIVE RELIGION. 3s. 6d.

GOUDGE, H. L., D.D.

THREE LECTURES ON THE EPISTLE TO THE EPHESIANS. 3s. 6d.

GREENWOOD, Alice Drayton, F.R.Hist.Soc.

HISTORY OF THE PEOPLE OF ENGLAND. The BEDE HISTORIES. Edited by Miss H. L. POWELL, St. Mary's College, Lancaster Gate.
    Vol. I.—55 B.C. to A.D. 1485. With 27 Illustrations and 15 Maps. 8s. 6d.
    Vol. II.—1485-1689. 7s. 6d.

HANDCOCK, P. S. P., M.A., Lecturer of the Palestine Exploration Fund.

THE LATEST LIGHT ON BIBLE LANDS. Second Edition, revised. With numerous Illustrations. 6s.

HARDEN, J. M., B.D., LL.D.

DICTIONARY OF THE VULGATE NEW TESTAMENT. 4s.

HARDWICK, John Charlton.

RELIGION AND SCIENCE. From Galileo to Bergson. 8s.

HARDY, Rev. T. J., M.A.

SPIRITISM IN THE LIGHT OF THE FAITH. A Comparison and a Contrast. 3s.

HASLEHURST, R. S. T., B.D.

THE PENITENTIAL DISCIPLINE OF THE EARLY CHURCH IN THE FIRST FOUR CENTURIES. 5s.

HIGGINBOTTOM, Sam, M.A.

THE GOSPEL AND THE PLOW; or, The Old Gospel and Modern Farming in Ancient India. 5s.

HOLLOWAY, Henry, M.A., B.D.

THE REFORMATION IN IRELAND. A Study of Ecclesiastical Legislation. 7s. 6d.

HOPE, The late Sir William St. John, Litt.D., Hon. D.C.L., Durham, and ATCHLEY, E. G. Cuthbert, F., L.R.C.P. Lond., M.R.C.S. Eng.

ENGLISH LITURGICAL COLOURS. With a Coloured Frontispiece. 25s.

ENGLISH LITURGICAL COLOURS, An Introduction to. 3s. 6d.

HUMPHREYS, Arthur James, B.A., D.D.

CHRISTIAN MORALS. Cloth boards. 4s.

JENKINSON, Wilberforce.

LONDON CHURCHES BEFORE THE GREAT FIRE. Illustrated by twenty reproductions in collotype, from old prints and drawings, by Mr. EMERY WALKER. 15s.

KELLY, The Rev. Alfred Davenport, M.A., Society of the Sacred Mission.

VALUES OF THE CHRISTIAN LIFE. With a Preface by the Right Rev. WILLIAM TEMPLE. 7s. 6d.

KIDD, B. J., D.D. (Editor).

DOCUMENTS ILLUSTRATIVE OF THE HISTORY OF THE CHURCH. To A.D. 313. 7s. 6d.

LUCE, A. A., M.C., B.D.

MONOPHYSITISM PAST AND PRESENT. 7s. 6d.

MACKEAN, W. H., D.D.

CHRISTIAN MONASTICISM IN EGYPT TO THE CLOSE OF THE FOURTH CENTURY. 8s.

MACLEAN, The Right Rev. Arthur J., D.D., Bishop of Moray, Ross, and Caithness.

RECENT DISCOVERIES ILLUSTRATING EARLY CHRISTIAN LIFE AND WORSHIP. Second Edition, revised. 2s. 6d.

MARTIN, Edward J., B.D., formerly Scholar of Oriel College, Oxford.

THE EMPEROR JULIAN. An Essay on his relations with the Christian Religion. 3s. 6d.

MAY, G. Lacey, M.A.

SOME EIGHTEENTH-CENTURY CHURCHMEN. Glimpses of English Church Life in the Eighteenth Century. With several Illustrations. 9s.

MERCER, The Right Rev. J. E., D.D.

THE PROBLEM OF CREATION. An attempt to define the Character and Trend of the Cosmic Process. 7s. 6d.

MINISTRY OF WOMEN, THE. A Report by a Committee appointed by the LORD ARCHBISHOP OF CANTERBURY. With Appendices and fifteen Collotype Illustrations. 12s. 6d.

MORISON, The Rev. E. F., D.D.

THE LORD'S PRAYER AND THE PRAYERS OF OUR LORD. A Scriptural Exposition. 3s. 6d.

MOZLEY, The Rev. J. K., B.D.

THE ACHIEVEMENTS OF CHRISTIANITY. 2s. 6d.

OESTERLEY, W. O. E., M.A., D.D.

IMMORTALITY AND THE UNSEEN WORLD. A study in Old Testament religion. 12s. 6d.

OESTERLEY, W. O. E., M.A., D.D., and BOX, G. H., M.A., D.D.

A SHORT SURVEY OF THE LITERATURE OF RABBINICAL AND MEDIÆVAL JUDAISM. 12s. 6d.

TRANSLATIONS OF EARLY DOCUMENTS. A Series of texts important for the study of Christian origins.

Twenty-four volumes of this series have now appeared. The *Book of Enoch* is the best known of the documents, but all deserve the attention of students.

PAGE, Jesse, F.R.G.S.

SCHWARTZ OF TANJORE. With Photogravure Frontispiece, Map, and six Illustrations. 7s. 6d.

PAKENHAM-WALSH, Herbert, D.D., Bishop in Assam.

DIVINE HEALING. Paper, 1s. 3d. ; cloth, 2s. 6d.

PARRY, The Right Rev. O. H., D.D., Bishop of Guiana.

THE PILGRIM IN JERUSALEM. With numerous Illustrations. 10s.

PEACOCK, Alice Evelyn, M.B.E.

THE DELIGHTFUL JOYS OF HEAVEN. 6s. 6d.

PEARCE, Ernest Harold, Litt.D., F.S.A., Bishop of Worcester.

WALTER DE WENLOK, Abbot of Westminster. With a Frontispiece. 12s.

POOLE, Reginald Lane.

ILLUSTRATIONS OF THE HISTORY OF MEDIÆVAL THOUGHT AND LEARNING. Second Edition, revised. 17s. 6d.

RELTON, Herbert M., D.D.

A STUDY IN CHRISTOLOGY. The Problem of the Relation of the Two Natures in the Person of Christ. Preface by the Rev. ARTHUR C. HEADLAM, D.D. 10s.

REICHEL, The Rev. O. J.

THE CANON LAW OF CHURCH INSTITUTIONS. Vol. I. 10s. 6d.

ROBINSON, J. Armitage, D.D., Dean of Wells.

BARNABAS, HERMAS AND THE DIDACHE. Being the Donnellan Lectures delivered before the University of Dublin in 1920. 6s.

ROBINSON, C. H., D.D., Editorial Secretary of the S.P.G.

HOW THE GOSPEL SPREAD THROUGH EUROPE. With Maps. Paper, 3s. 6d. ; cloth, 5s.

ROGERS, The Rev. Clement F., M.A.

WHY MEN BELIEVE. The Groundwork of Apologetics. 2s. 6d.

ROLT, The late C. E.

THE SPIRITUAL BODY. Edited with an Introduction by W. J. SPARROW SIMPSON, D.D. 6s.

SANDERS, E. K.

JACQUES BENIGNE BOSSUET. With two Photogravure Portraits. 15s.
SAINTE CHANTAL. 1572–1641. A Study in Vocation. 10s. 6d.

SCOTT, Melville, D.D.

THE MESSAGE OF HOSEA. With Preface by the DEAN OF LICHFIELD. 8s. 6d.

SHEBBEARE, The Rev. Charles J., M.A.

THE CHALLENGE OF THE UNIVERSE. A popular restatement of the Argument from Design. 7s. 6d.

SIMPSON, W. J. Sparrow, D.D.

THE LETTERS OF ST. AUGUSTINE. 10s.
FRENCH CATHOLICS IN THE NINETEENTH CENTURY. 5s.

SNOWDEN, P. L., Vicar of Hepworth.

THE ATONEMENT AND OURSELVES. 10s. 6d.

STANTON, The Rev. H. U. Weitbrecht, Ph.D., D.D.

THE TEACHING OF THE QUR'AN. With an Account of its Growth, and a Subject Index. 7s.

STEWART, The Rev. D. A., M.A.

THE PLACE OF CHRISTIANITY AMONG THE GREATER RELIGIONS OF THE WORLD. 7s. 6d.

STOKES, The Rev. H. P., LL.D., Litt.D., F.S.A.
A SHORT HISTORY OF THE JEWS IN ENGLAND. With eight Illustrations. 5s. 6d.

STURGE, M. Carta, Moral Sciences Tripos, Cambridge.
THEOSOPHY AND CHRISTIANITY. A Comparison. Second Edition. 2s.

SWEET, Charles F.
NEW LIFE IN THE OLDEST EMPIRE. [Japan.] 6s.

SWETE, The late Rev. Henry Barclay, D.D., D.Litt.
THE LIFE OF THE WORLD TO COME. With a Portrait. 3s.

SWINSTEAD, The Rev. J. Howard, D.D.
THE SWEDISH CHURCH AND OURS. With two Illustrations. 6s. 6d.

WATSON, Herbert A., D.D.
THE INCARNATION AND PERSONALITY. 9s.

WESTLAKE, H. F., M.A., F.S.A.
THE PARISH GILDS OF MEDIÆVAL ENGLAND. With six Illustrations. 15s.

WILLIAMS, The Rev. N. P.
THE FIRST EASTER MORNING. Paper, 2s. 6d. ; Cloth, 3s. 6d.

WILSON, The Rev. James M., D.D., Canon and Vice-Dean.
THE WORCESTER LIBER ALBUS. Glimpses of Life in a Great Benedictine Monastery in the Fourteenth Century. With a collotype facsimile. 15s.

WOOD, Percival, M.R.C.S., L.R.C.P.
MOSES : THE FOUNDER OF PREVENTIVE MEDICINE. 4s.

WRIGHT, The Rev. Leslie, M.A., B.D.
THE EUCHARISTIC OFFICE OF THE BOOK OF COMMON PRAYER. 3s. 6d.

YOUNG, The Rev. P. N. F., M.A., and FERRERS, Agnes.
INDIA IN CONFLICT. 3s. 6d.

ZWEMER, Samuel M., F.R.G.S.
THE INFLUENCE OF ANIMISM ON ISLAM. An account of popular superstition. With twelve Illustrations. 10s.

SOCIETY for PROMOTING CHRISTIAN KNOWLEDGE

S.P.C.K. House, Northumberland Avenue, London, W.C. 2.